Arthur Lockwood Wagner

Elements of Military Science

Arthur Lockwood Wagner

Elements of Military Science

ISBN/EAN: 9783337035280

Printed in Europe, USA, Canada, Australia, Japan

Cover: Foto ©Suzi / pixelio.de

More available books at **www.hansebooks.com**

CONTENTS.

	Page.
PREFACE	5

ORGANIZATION AND TACTICS:—

Organization and Discipline	9
Characteristics of the Three Arms	24
Infantry in Attack and Defense	33
Cavalry in Attack and Defense	58
Artillery in Attack and Defense	70
The Three Arms Combined	83

THE SERVICE OF SECURITY AND INFORMATION:—

The Advance Guard	99
Outposts in General	110
Sentinels and Pickets. Supports, Reserve. The Outpost at Night	121
Outpost Patrols. How Outposts are Posted and Relieved,	136
Reconnaissance—Kinds of Patrols	144
Duties of the Patrol—Special Cases of Reconnoitering	151
Duties of the Patrol—Indications of the Enemy	160
Reports—Special Patrols. Cavalry Patrols. The Cavalry Screen	167
Rear Guards	181

FIELD FORTIFICATION. MARCHES. SUPPLY:—

Field Fortification	197
Marches and Supply	207

PREFACE.

This little book is intended primarily for the students of such of our colleges as enjoy the services of instructors detailed from the Army. It is intended, therefore, for pupils who are not familiar with that complicated machine, a modern army. Hence an attempt has been made to present plainly and clearly, under the form of question and answer, the main points of the art military. It has been thought best to omit the subject of Strategy, as that is essentially a study for generals rather than for soldiers and subordinate commanders.

Resting, as this book does, on "Organization and Tactics" and "The Service of Security and Information," it is thought that the instructor can draw upon these sources for such illustrations, historical and other, as he may think suited to the requirements of his classes. By following this course, the pupil will have before him at all times the essential principles, while their application and illustration will be furnished by his instructor. For the section on Fortifications I am indebted to the "Manual of Military Field Engineering," prepared at the United States Infantry and Cavalry School.

I wish here to express my thanks to First Lieutenant C. DeW. Willcox, 7th Artillery, for valuable assistance in the preparation of the following pages; indeed, a great part of the preparation of the work has been delegated to him.

ARTHUR L. WAGNER,
Lieut.-Colonel and Assistant Adjutant-General.

PART I.

Organization and Tactics.

CHAPTER 1.

ORGANIZATION AND DISCIPLINE.

Q. State the two great divisions of the Art of War, and define each.

A. Strategy and Tactics. Strategy is the art of moving an army in the theater of war, with a view to placing it in such a position relative to the enemy as to increase the probability of victory, to increase the consequences of victory, or to lessen the consequences of defeat. Tactics is the art of disposing and maneuvering troops on the field of battle.

Q. State and define other subdivisions of the Art of War.

A. Logistics and Military Engineering. Of these the former comprises everything relating to the movement and supply of armies, and the latter all that pertains to fortification and to siege operations.

Q. What subdivisions of Tactics are often made?

A. Minor Tactics and Grand Tactics; the first relating to the movements of small bodies and to the tactics of the respective arms, while the latter includes the combination of the several arms and the handling of armies in battles. Tactics may also be divided into Maneuver Tactics and Fighting Tactics; the first dealing with movements by which troops are brought into position on the battle-field, and the second with formations of attack and defense, and with the handling of troops in acutal battle.

Q. Why should Organization and Tactics be considered together?

A. Strategy is largely independent of all details of organization, arms, etc., of the army, but Tactics varies with all such details. For this reason Organization and Tactics should be treated together.

Q. Define tactical organization.

A. Tactical organization is the arrangement of an army for the purpose of obtaining its most prompt and powerful action in response to the will of the commander.

The Line.

(a) Infantry.

Q. Upon what unit should the organization of an army be based?

A. Upon the largest body of troops that can be directly commanded by a single leader, and at the same time be able to appear in close order on the battle-field without risk of quickly incurring ruinous losses from the enemy's fire. This unit is known as the "tactical unit," and in our service is the battalion.

Q. What is the best organization for our infantry?

A. All things considered, the best organization for our infantry calls for companies of one hundred men each, formed into battalions of four companies. This organization is in accord with our own war experience and with the conditions of the modern battle-field.

Q. Give the subdivisions of the battalion down to and including the squad.

A. We have first the company under the command of a captain; the company itself is divided into two platoons, each under the command of a lieutenant; the platoon breaks up into two sections, each under a sergeant; and finally the sections are divided into squads of eight men each.

Q. What organization is the administrative unit, and why is it so regarded?

A. The administrative unit is the regiment. Three (sometimes four) battalions form the regiment. This is both a tactical and an administrative unit. Tactically it is a necessity, for a brigadier general can easily command three regiments where he would find the control of nine battalions a matter of much difficulty.

Q. What is the composition of the brigade?

A. The brigade is the largest organization composed exclusively of infantry. In the United States Army it consists of three regiments, and has therefore a strength in round numbers of 3600 rifles. Though made up of only one arm of the service, it almost invariably acts in conjunction with the other arms.

(b) Artillery.

Q. What is the tactical unit of the artillery, and how many guns does this unit contain?

A. The tactical unit of the artillery is the battery; it usually contains six guns.

Q. How is artillery united into larger organizations?

A. Into battalions of two, three, or four batteries; the battalion of four batteries being the best. The regiment of artillery is a purely administrative unit.

(c) Cavalry.

Q. What is the tactical unit of cavalry in our own and in foreign services?

A. In most armies the tactical unit of cavalry is the squadron of 150 sabers. In the United States Army the squadron has a war strength, in round numbers, of 400 sabers, and is divided into four troops.

It is our tactical unit, and as such is particularly important in respect of dismounted action.

Q. In our cavalry, what kind of organization is the regiment, and of what does it consist?

A. In our service the cavalry regiment has three squadrons, and is both an administrative and a tactical organization. It is the largest cavalry organization entirely independent of the other arms.

Q. What is the organization of foreign cavalry regiments?

A. In the French and German armies, the regiment has five squadrons of 150 men each; four of these go into the field, the fifth being retained as a regimental *dépôt*.

Q. State the composition of the cavalry brigade, division, and corps.

A. The cavalry brigade consists of three regiments, and should have a battery of horse artillery attached to it; the cavalry division consists of three brigades of cavalry and of a battalion of horse artillery, while the cavalry corps has three divisions and at least six batteries of horse artillery. At full strength the corps would have in round numbers 33,000 men, but so great a force of cavalry would very rarely be united into one body.

(d) *The Three Arms Combined.*

Q. State the composition of an infantry division.

A. The infantry division is generally composed of all arms of the service, but is known as an "infantry" division, not only because its proportion of that arm is greater than that of any other, but also as a means of distinguishing it from a division composed of cavalry and horse artillery. The infantry division is an admin-

Organization and Discipline. 13

istrative as well as tactical organization; it consists of three brigades of infantry, numbered in each division as 1st, 2d, and 3d, and a number of cavalry troops and batteries, varying according to circumstances. Of artillery, the best proportion is generally a battalion of four batteries. The cavalry attached to a division is known as the "divisional cavalry."

Q. What kind of unit is the army corps, and what should it constitute?

A. The army corps is the *strategical* unit. It should be complete in all its parts and constitute an army in itself, capable of acting independently at any time, and always able to act promptly as a whole.

Q. What is the composition of an army corps?

A. The fighting strength of the army corps consists of three divisions (numbered in each corps as the 1st, 2d, and 3d), one or more regiments of cavalry, and the corps artillery.

Q. How is the command of the corps artillery exercised?

A. The corps artillery is under the control of the corps commander, and under the immediate orders of the chief of artillery of the corps, being independent of the divisional artillery. It may, however, be united to the latter. The corps artillery consists of a brigade of two battalions each.

Q. What is the ordinary strength of an army corps in round numbers?

A. The size of the corps is practically the same in all armies, being everywhere approximately 30,000 men.

Q. What considerations govern the strength of an army corps?

A. A corps of 30,000 men marching on a single road —the usual case—forms a column about fifteen miles long. Its rear is consequently a day's march from the head of the column. A greater strength would therefore make the column so long that its head might be defeated before the rear could arrive on the field. The strength assumed may therefore be regarded as a maximum. Considerations of marching and of deployment make it undesirable to have a corps of smaller size.

Q. What considerations govern in the grouping of army corps into armies?

A. An "army" should consist of not fewer than three nor more than six army corps. An army of more than six corps has been shown by experience to be unwieldy; if of fewer than three corps, then the necessity of having a reserve causes the unity of one of these to be broken up.

Q. Upon what does the question of the proportion of the three arms depend?

A. Upon the nature of the theater of operations, the composition of the enemy's forces, the special adaptability of the people of the country to one arm rather than to another, and even on the casualties of the campaign.

Q. State the rule for the proportion of artillery in general, and also under unfavorable circumstances.

A. Generally from three to four guns for every 1000 men of the other arms. This proportion would, however, have to be reduced in difficult, thickly wooded, or mountainous country, or, indeed, in any country where the roads are few and poor. While the proportion of guns to infantry cannot be definitely fixed, it may be safely prescribed that the guns with an army should be as many as can be promptly brought upon the field of battle and effectively used there.

Q. How does the proportion of cavalry vary, and what should be the rule with us?

A. The proportion of cavalry to the other arms varies exceedingly. In our own case it ought to be such as to enable our cavalry speedily to overwhelm any to which it may be opposed, no matter what the proportion may be to the other arms.

(e) Special Troops.

Q. What are special troops?

A. Those of the Engineer and of the Signal Corps, and of the Medical and of the Quartermaster Departments.

Q. What are the duties of engineer troops in the United States Army?

A. They perform the duties of sappers and miners, and of pontoneers.

Q. How should the bridge train of our army be organized and handled?

A. Each of our corps should have a battalion of engineer troops, and a bridge train capable of spanning a stream 300 yards wide. This corps train should, as a rule, be kept intact, with provision for uniting the trains of the several corps under the chief engineer of the army whenever expedient.

Q. State the strength, duties, and equipment of the signal troops with an army corps.

A. The signal corps is charged with the management of the field telegraph, of the military balloons, and with the service of signalling generally. A company of 5 officers and of 175 men should be attached to each corps, and should be provided with material for 50 miles of portable telegraph line.

Q. State the sanitary organization of a division and its duties.

A. The sanitary organization of a division consists of one bearer company, one ambulance company, and one field hospital with accommodations for 500 patients, a total strength of 44 medical officers and 274 men, distributed among the respective units in proportion to their relative strength. The bearer company establishes a dressing-station and carries the wounded to it. Here these receive such attendance as is necessary before their removal to a field hospital. The ambulance company conveys the wounded to the field hospitals.

Q. Enumerate the medical staff of a corps.

A. Each corps has a medical director and a reserve of men and of material sufficient to expand the capacity of the field hospitals to at least 2000 patients.

Q. Describe the purpose and position of general hospitals.

A. These are hospitals quite in the rear of the army, or at the base of operations, to which the sick and wounded are sent for extended treatment.

Q. What is the method employed in the United States Army for the military police of the army?

A. Troops are detailed for duty as provost guard, preference being given to regiments and battalions that have suffered severely in action. The provost guard of an army corps is of varying size, but rarely exceeds a full battalion or a depleted regiment.

The Train.

Q. What is the amount of ammunition with which

the infantry should be promptly supplied, and how is it carried?

A. The infantry should have at least 200 rounds per man; of these, 100 are carried on the person, 64 in the small-arm ammunition wagon, and the remainder in the ammunition columns.

Q. What is the amount of ammunition carried for the field batteries?

A. For each field battery 231 rounds per gun are carried, as follows: 42 in each limber, and 126 in each of the nine caissons, the remainder being with the ammunition columns.

Q. What is the amount of ammunition carried for the horse batteries?

A. 231 rounds per gun, 168 being with the batteries and the remainder with the ammunition columns.

Q. How is the ammunition column commanded, how divided, and to what is it attached?

A. The ammunition column is under the command of an artillery officer, and is attached to the corps artillery. It is divided into four sections, one for each division and one for the corps artillery.

Q. What is the organization of the corps train, and what does it carry?

A. The corps train carries five days' supplies of rations and of forage. It should ordinarily be divided into four parts, three provision columns and one forage column.

Q. What does the baggage train carry?

A. The necessary camp equipage of the several headquarters.

Q. What is the total transportation of an army corps at full strength?

—2—

A. More than 1000 wagons and more than 5000 animals, exclusive of wagons and caissons attached to batteries.

Q. By whom should the service of the train be performed?

A. By trained quartermaster's men; if these are not available, then by hired civilians or by details from the line.

The Staff.

Q. What are the principal duties of a commanding general, and how is he relieved of a part of them?

A. The commanding general is charged with the maintenance of the efficiency of his army and with the proper conduct of military operations, and his responsibility extends to a multitude of details, the personal supervision of which is beyond the powers of any one man—*e. g.*, supply, equipment, the preparation and prompt communication of orders, etc. These details are attended to by his staff, and on the quality of the staff of an army depends in the highest degree its efficiency.

Q. State the duties and responsibilities of the chief of staff.

A. The chief of staff gives expression in written orders to the will of the commander, and attends to all his military correspondence. He is responsible for all the details involved in the general instructions of the commanding general, relative to the marching, camping, and security of the army; he sees to it that all orders given are properly carried out, and must be prepared at any moment to give his chief an accurate account of the numbers, position, and condition of the general command.

Q. What officers should be under the command of

the chief of staff, and what is meant by the military staff?

A. The chief of staff should have under his command such officers of the Adjutant-General's and of the Inspector-General's departments as may be necessary members of the commander's staff. These, with the *aides-de-camp* of the commanding general, the chief of artillery, the chief or inspector of cavalry, the chief engineer, the chief signal officer, and the provost marshal general, make up the military as distinguished from the administrative staff.

Q. What are the duties of the provost marshal?

A. He preserves proper police in the army, protects the inhabitants from pillage and violence, arrests stragglers and deserters, controls camp-followers, and has charge of prisoners and of deserters. He is in addition the chief of the secret service and the commanding officer of the provost guard.

Q. What are the duties of the chief signal officer, and of the chiefs of artillery and of cavalry, and of the chief engineer?

A. The chief signal officer has charge of the military telegraph, of signal stations, and of balloons, and commands the signal troops.

The chief of artillery has general charge of the artillery material of the army, is inspector of artillery, and is the principal assistant of the commanding general in all that relates to his arm. He does not command, except when the artillery of two or more corps is combined in action.

The chief of cavalry should be in active command of all the cavalry of the army, and should habitually remain in person with the force under his command.

The chief engineer officer has duties analogous to

those of the chief of artillery. He has general charge of all engineer operations on a large scale.

Q. Enumerate the officers of the administrative staff, and state the duties of each.

A. As the name implies, the administrative staff has charge of general questions of administration, supply, and equipment. It is made up of:

The judge-advocate at the headquarters of the army, who has general supervision of the proceedings of courts-martial and of courts of inquiry, etc.

The commissary of musters, who makes all musters into and out of the service, and exercises general supervision over all muster- and pay-rolls.

The chief ordnance officer, who is charged with the supply of arms, ammunition, equipment, etc., for all three arms.

The chief quartermaster, who is responsible for forage, transportation, clothing, camp and garrison equipage, and for the management of trains.

The chief commissary of subsistence, who has charge of the food-supply of the army.

The chief paymaster, who pays the army.

The medical director, who has charge of the hospital and ambulance service, and of everything relating to the care of the sick and wounded.

Q. Of what officers are staffs of an army corps and of a division composed?

A. Of approximately the same officers as those of the staff of an army. They are reduced in number, however, in the ratio of the lesser importance of their duties, as determined by the smaller number of men they have to deal with.

Q. Give the composition of an infantry division, and of an army corps.

THE DIVISION.

	Officers.	Medical Officers.	Non-Commissioned Officers and Privates.			Aggregate.	Guns.	Other Carriages.	Horses.	Mules.	Total Animals.
			Combatants.	Non-Combatants.	Total.						
C. O. and Staff..	11	1	....	22	22	34	..	3	28	18	46
Three Infantry Brigades.....	405	30	11142	222	11364	11799	...	69	258	378	636
Four Batteries..	22	4	703	4	707	733	24	44	635	...	635
Bearer Co	...	3	.	60	60	63	...	4	12	12	24
Ambulance Co..	...	3	....	72	72	75	...	53	118	18	136
Field Hospital .	...	3	....	40	40	43	...	7	12	30	42
Grand Total..	438	44	11845	420	12265	12747	24	180	1063	456	1519

THE ARMY CORPS.

	Officers.	Medical Officers.	Non-Commissioned Officers and Privates.			Aggregate.	Guns.	Other Carriages.	Horses.	Mules.	Total Animals.
			Combatants.	Non-Combatants.	Total.						
C. O. and Staff ..	15	1	....	31	31	47	...	6	37	36	73
Three Divisions..	1314	132	35535	1260	36795	38241	72	540	3189	1368	4557
Corps Artillery ..	48	8	1409	8	1417	1473	48	88	1386	....	1386
Cavalry ..	48	3	1239	28	1267	1313	...	7	1359	40	1399
Engineers.	19	1	601	7	608	628	...	58	12	338	350
Signal Corps...	5	1	...	175	175	181	...	9	38	..	38
Hospital Reserve.	....	3	....	40	40	43	...	7	12	30	42
Ammunition Col.	10	2	... .	350	350	362	...	121	332	420	752
Supply Train....	24	2	....	774	774	800	...	469	153	2814	2967
Horse Dépôt...	3	...	....	100	100	103	...	1	106	100	206
Grand Total .	1431	153	38784	2773	41557	43191	120	1306	6624	5146	11770

Q. What is the difference between the "fighting strength" and the "ration strength" of a corps?

A. By "fighting strength" is meant all the men exclusive of officers who take position in the line of battle and fight; the "ration strength" is equal to the sum of the "fighting strength" and the non-combatants.

Q. State the proper rank of the commanders of the different organizations.

A. Of a company, troop, or battery...captain
battalion.........................major
regiment..........................colonel
brigade...................brigadier-general
division.....................major-general
army corps................lieutenant-general
army.............................general.
aggregation of armies........general-in-chief,
        generalissimo, or captain-general

Q. What is the necessity for recruitment?

A. Losses from whatsoever source begin with the campaign itself, and generally reach a maximum at the time of the severest fighting, which is also the period of greatest fatigue and hardship. Stragglers and deserters also help in reducing the strength of an army. Hence the necessity of recruiting from the very outset.

Q. Give the two general methods of recruiting an army.

A. First, by replacing losses in each regiment by recruits from its own *dépôt;* second, by adding new regiments to the army.

The first system prevails in Europe, and is undoubtedly the better. The second system was generally employed in the United States during the Civil War, and was pernicious in the extreme.

Q. Define discipline.

A. Discipline is that quality possessed by efficient soldiers which causes each to appreciate and accept without question the powers and limitations of his rank; which inspires each with confidence in the military steadfastness of his comrades, and makes obedience to his lawful superiors a second nature. The object of discipline is in every case the same: to cause the army to respond to the will of the commander.

Q. What two general methods are there for promoting discipline, and which is the better?

A. Rewards and punishments; and of these the former is the better. In practice both are utilized.

Q. What are the best evidences of true discipline?

A. The unmurmuring endurance of hardships by the soldiers and their willing, energetic, and persistent efforts to perform their whole duty in the presence of the enemy, a minimum of stragglers on the march and of skulkers in battle, are the best proof of good discipline.

CHAPTER II.

CHARACTERISTICS OF THE THREE ARMS.

Q. State the powers and limitations of infantry.

A. Both numerically and in the effects of its action the infantry is the most important part of the army. It can operate on all kinds of ground, is equally adapted to offensive and to defensive action, and can act either at a halt or in motion. It is, however, limited to the pace of the individual man, and its action is confined to the range of the rifle.

Q. Describe the arms and action of infantry.

A. Its weapons are the rifle and bayonet; its action, fire, shock, and a combination of these two. Of these, fire-action is the most important, but it must be supplemented, in general, by real or threatened shock. Actual shock is very rare.

Q. What is the pace of infantry?

A. At drill, 100 yards to the minute; on the march, about 88 yards a minute; in double time, this pace is increased to 147 yards a minute. The marching pace of infantry, in good condition on good roads, is 3 miles an hour, or, including halts, from 2.5 to 2.75 miles an hour. The state of the weather, the nature of the roads, and other conditions beyond human control, may greatly reduce this rate.

Q. State the essential qualities of infantry.

A. The value of infantry depends on the effectiveness of its fire-action, and on its ability to avoid destructive losses from the fire of the enemy. Hence the infantry soldier must be carefully trained in fire disci-

Q. What are the weapons of the trooper in the United States and in Europe?

A. In the United States, the saber, magazine carbine, and revolver; in Europe, the lance is generally added and the revolver discarded.

Q. What is the pace of cavalry under varying conditions?

A.

The walk.................................4 miles an hour.
Maneuvering trot....................8 miles an hour.
Slow trot..................................6 to 6.5 miles an hour.
Alternate trot and walk...........5 miles an hour.
Maneuvering gallop...............12 miles an hour.
Alternate trot and gallop........10 miles an hour.
Full gallop..............................16 miles an hour.

Q. State the powers and limitations of cavalry.

A. It can rapidly transport itself to the point where it is needed, and can take advantage of opportunities that would vanish before the infantry could strike; it can check an enemy by its manifest readiness to strike; it can perform reconnaissance work wholly impossible for infantry, and without it adequate pursuit is out of the question. It is, however, a very costly arm, costing as it does three times as much as the infantry, and its use on the field of battle is rarer than that of the other two arms.

Q. Into what is artillery primarily divided?

A. Into heavy and into light.

Q. Define each of these.

A. Heavy artillery embraces all the guns used in siege operations or in batteries of position; the latter being batteries of heavy guns used on the battle-field to defend or to attack very important points, and in which mobility is sacrificed to destructive power.

Light artillery comprises horse, field, and mountain batteries.

Q. For what is horse artillery specially designed, and what is its essential characteristic?

A. For service with cavalry; and therefore its essential characteristic is mobility. The cannoneers are consequently mounted. In our service it is armed with a 3.2-inch breech-loading rifle.

Q. What kinds of batteries are included in field artillery?

A. Heavy field and light field; the former, in the United States, having the 3.6-inch gun, and the latter the 3.2-inch. In this sort of artillery the cannoneers march by the guns, or else are mounted on the ammunition chests or axle seats.

Q. Describe mountain batteries.

A. These are for use in mountainous regions or in regions where the roads are bad and traction difficult. In our service the gun used is the Hotchkiss mountain rifle, 1.65-inch caliber.

Q. What are the arms of artillery?

A. The gun is the special arm of the artillery. The sergeants are armed with the saber and revolver, and the other men with the revolver and knife.

Q. What is the pace of artillery under various conditions?

A. The same as that of cavalry. In the field the trot is the maneuvering pace, the gallop being exceptional. Horse artillery gallops whenever cavalry would have to gallop.

Q. State the powers and limitations of artillery.

A. It is the only arm that can destroy material objects at a distance, and is largely independent of the personal factor, as its action is at a distance from the guns. It is incapable of independent action, and is limited to fire-action, and this only when at a halt in battery. Like the cavalry, it is expensive and hard to train. From its nature it is bulky, taking up a great deal of space on the march. Lastly, it can be neutralized by the destruction of its *matériel* as well as by that of its *personnel*.

Q. What is the range of field artillery, and into what zones is it divided?

A. Under favorable conditions, good results may be expected at 3 miles; but, as a rule, 3000 yards may be taken as the extreme effective range. From this point to the enemy, the field, in respect of range, may be regarded as composed of three zones: (1) long range, from 3000 to 2000 yards; within this zone artillery is effective and has but little to fear from infantry fire; (2) medium range, 2000 to 800 yards; the fire-effect of artillery increases, but it is seriously exposed to the hostile artillery; (3) short range, within 800 yards; artillery should not be used within this range, unless its annihilation by infantry fire is justified by the effect to be produced.

Q. State the kinds of artillery fire, and describe each.

A. Direct fire, from guns using service charges, the angle of elevation being less than 15 degrees;

Indirect or curved fire, from guns using reduced charges, and from mortars and howitzers at any angle less than 15 degrees;

High-angle fire, from guns, mortars, and howitzers, at any angle greater than 15 degrees;

Frontal fire, in which the line of fire is perpendicular to the hostile front;

Oblique fire, in which the line of fire is oblique to the hostile front;

Enfilade fire, from guns in the prolongation of the enemy's line; if this fire sweeps the front of a defensive line, it is called flanking fire;

Reverse fire, on the rear of the enemy;

Cross fire, in which the projectiles from guns in different positions cross one another's paths on or in front of the enemy's line.

Q. Give the classification of shell, and describe each.

A. Shell are divided into common and torpedo. Common shell are hollow cast-iron or steel cylinders with ogival heads, closed at the end and filled with powder. Torpedo shell are filled with guncotton or other high explosive.

Q. Describe the shrapnel.

A. The shrapnel is a hollow projectile filled with bullets, and has a bursting charge only just powerful enough to burst the envelope and release the bullets; these then go on with the velocity of the projectile at the moment of burst.

Q. Describe the canister.

A. Canister is a tin cylinder filled with bullets, kept in place by filling the interstices with sand, sawdust, etc. The cylinder is broken by the shock of discharge, and the bullets then scatter. It is an obsolescent projectile.

Q. State the kinds and uses of fuses.

A. Fuses are used to burst the shell and shrapnel. There are three kinds:

1. Time fuse, ignited by the discharge of the piece, and so arranged as to burn a certain predetermined

length of time before the fire reaches the bursting charge;

2. Percussion fuse, igniting the bursting charge by the shock of impact;

3. Combination fuse, possessing the properties of the two others.

Q. When should common shell be used?

A. They should be used to destroy parapets, houses, and in general against all material objects; they are also of value against troops in mass, and, in trial shots, to determine the range. They are effective at 4000 yards.

Q. When should torpedo or mine shell be used?

A. Against troops under cover.

Q. When and how should shrapnel be used?

A. Against troops in all formations, in the open or under shelter. It is *the* projectile against flesh and blood. Effective at 3000 yards, at 1100 and under its effects are absolutely annihilating if the field be open and the guns skilfully used. It is burst in the air by a time fuse.

Q. Define the term "rapid-fire" gun.

A. A rapid-fire gun is any single-barrelled gun using fixed ammunition—that is, ammunition in which the projectile, charge, and primer are so combined that only one motion is necessary in loading.

Q. Define the term "machine gun," and state to what use these guns may be put.

A. A machine gun is any combination of breech-loading rifled barrels, using fixed ammunition, grouped about an axis or else disposed horizontally, and loaded and fired in succession by a suitable mechanical contrivance at the breech, the empty cartridges being automatically ejected.

Q. How may these guns be employed?

A. They should be placed in separate batteries, not pitted against artillery; they form, however, a part of the general artillery command. They are frequently valuable to cavalry on raids, and to the defensive in holding advanced posts, in flanking fronts, etc., but to the offensive their use is doubtful.

Q. What two kinds of cover may be obtained for field guns?

A. Artificial and natural. Natural cover is any feature of the ground that will intercept or turn a projectile, or so conceal the pieces as to deceive the enemy in respect of the range. Artificial cover consists of ordinary intrenchments, of gun-pits, and of portable shields.

CHAPTER III.

INFANTRY IN ATTACK AND IN DEFENSE.

Q. What is the object of the attack?

A. The forcible expulsion of the enemy from his position. Fire-action alone cannot accomplish this; hence a successful attack implies the ability to reach the defender's position. The object, therefore, of an attack formation is to arrange and move troops so as to escape destructive losses, and to reach the hostile position with a force superior or at least equal to that of the enemy.

Q. What conditions should an attack formation satisfy?

A. 1. It should enable the troops to make the most effective use of the rifle.

2. It should present the least favorable target to the enemy, and allow advantage to be taken of the sheltering features of the ground.

3. It should admit celerity of movement, so as to shorten the period of exposure to the hostile fire.

4. It should enable the attack to deliver a shock at the end of the fire-action.

Q. How are the first two conditions satisfied?

A. By a firing line of skirmishers or of squads at suitable intervals, supported by troops belonging to the same battalion.

Q. What should the front of the firing line be equal to?

A. It should be equal to the front of the battalion in close order. The extreme firing front of a battalion in a regiment should not exceed one and a half times the front of the battalion in close order. In general the maximum front is regulated by the necessity of control by the battalion commander; the minimum, by the requirement that each man must have room enough to use his rifle with effect.

Q. How are losses in the firing line replaced?

A. By a portion of the battalion following as a *support*, at such distance and in such formation as to reinforce the firing line readily without incurring serious losses itself. As the action proceeds, the distance between these two bodies decrease until the support is finally absorbed.

Q. How are the flanks of the firing line protected?

A. By the reserve. Equal in numbers to the firing line and the support combined, the reserve is a body held in hand for use on either flank or at any part of the line that may be pierced by a counter-thrust of the enemy.

Q. As the attack approaches the firing line, what becomes of the reserve?

A. It is merged in the firing line.

Q. Is the advance of the reserve sufficient to carry forward the firing line to the final assault?

A. As a rule, not. In general a second line has to be called on, and even a third line is sometimes required to clinch the results of attack.

Q. Give the main divisions of an attacking force.

A. It is divided primarily into firing line, support, and reserve. The first two make up the fighting line, and the fighting line with the reserve constitute the first line. This first line is generally supported by a second line, and these two together by a third.

Infantry in Attack and in Defense.   35

Q. How have the functions of the skirmish line changed, what difficulty has arisen in consequence, and what measures have to be taken to correct it?

A. The skirmish line, formerly used to feel and to develop the enemy or to cover a deployment, has now become the most important element, not only beginning the action, but carrying it on to the end. As skirmishers are harder to control than the same number of men would be if in close order, there has resulted an increased difficulty of command joined to a tendency on the part of the men to get out of hand and to waste their ammunition. These difficulties are remedied in a certain degree by a subdivision of the company into squads, by stringent discipline, and by careful instruction in fire discipline.

Q. Define fire discipline, and give the five rules required by it.

A. Fire discipline is the instinctive habit, developed in the men by instruction and training, of commencing or ceasing or relaxing the fire, or of concentrating it upon a defined object, all in obedience to the will of the commander. Hence the following rules:

Never fire except when ordered, and then only the number of cartridges indicated.

Never fire after the command or signal "Cease firing."

Never fire except at the named objective.

Never fail to adjust the sight at the range named.

Always aim at the feet of the enemy.

Q. Is the observance of these simple rules easy in action?

A. No; for in the excitement of battle the men become so absorbed in the act of firing that they perform the motions automatically rather than intelligently, and seem to be actuated by a desire to fire rapidly rather than with effect.

Q. Why is long-range fire generally to be deprecated?

A. Because it might lead to exhaustion of ammunition before reaching the most effective ranges.

Q. When may long-range fire be forced on an assailant?

A. When the enemy uses it with effect, under which circumstances troops become demoralized unless allowed to return it. It should stop, though, when the reasons for its employment have ceased to exist.

Q. When long-range fire is used by the assailant, what troops should be charged with replying to it, and what target should these troops select?

A. Troops in close order, firing against masses of the enemy if possible.

Q. How close should the attacking infantry advance before opening fire, and how close can it usually advance?

A. If possible, the attacking infantry should advance to within 500 yards of the enemy before opening fire. It is rarely the case, however, that infantry can get up to 700—800 yards without being compelled to open fire. This latter limit it ought to reach, though, if its morale is good and it is well supported by its own artillery.

Q. How must the attacking infantry obtain protection at the longer ranges?

A. From its own artillery, which is expected to keep down the hostile artillery fire, and in any case to divert it from the advancing infantry.

Q. State why volley firing is desirable, the objections to it, when it is possible, and what should be done when the men are disconcerted.

A. Volley firing is desirable, because the men are more easily kept in hand, the expenditure of ammunition is more easily regulated, the objective of fire can be changed at any moment, and the effect on the enemy is more demoralizing than that of fire at will. On the other hand, the leader is not sure that each man has finished aiming, and the quick command to fire is calculated to cause an impulsive pull of the trigger and so derange the aim. At very close quarters independent fire is more advantageous.

Volley firing is possible only when the men are cool enough to understand and obey orders. When it is noticed that the men are disconcerted, and are firing ragged volleys, the fire at will should be ordered.

Q. What must be the state of discipline if good results are to flow from volley firing?

A. The men must be so trained as to fire only the number of cartridges indicated, and will, if the number be not indicated, cease firing on hearing the signal to that effect.

Q. When should rapid fire begin, and what should then be done?

A. Rapid fire should, if possible, be postponed until just before the final assault. At this point bayonets should be fixed, and as intense a fire as possible be directed straight to the front.

Q. How is protection from the enemy's fire to be sought at the shorter ranges, and what conditions must cover fulfill?

A. Protection must be sought in the use of natural cover, such as ditches, trees, folds of the ground, etc.; if there be no natural cover, the men must lie down. In all cases the cover chosen must be such that the men sheltered by it can see the enemy, and have an effective fire on him.

Q. In regard to cover, what two things should the men be taught?

A. Not only to take advantage of it, but to leave it on an order to that effect.

Q. Why are the rushes made, what regulates their distance, and how are they made?

A. Whenever the enemy's fire permits, the advance should be uninterrupted. But on arriving within 500—600 yards of the hostile position, the fire is so hot that even if the remaining space were passed over in double time, the men would be swept out of existence. Even if they were not, they would be so winded that they could not engage in the hand-to-hand conflict. The space is therefore covered by the succession of rushes or bounds. These give the men an opportunity to recover their wind, to protect themselves by such cover as may be available, and to diminish the effects of the hostile fire by the intensity of their own. Generally the length of a rush should be from 30 to 50 yards, and it may be made either by the entire line or by a fraction of it. The latter is the better method, as the advance of a fraction is covered by the fire of its neighbors.

Q. Why should the fractions of the line alternating in rushes be large?

A. If small, the front of fire will be too restricted, and there will be danger of the troops in front receiving fire from their own men in rear.

Q. At the opening of the fight what proportion of the men should be in the firing line?

A. Generally not more than one-fourth. The rifle is most effectively handled when the skirmish line consists of one man to each yard of front.

Q. Why should great care be taken to give the proper direction to the firing line when it first moves to the attack?

A. Because a change of direction under a heavy fire is always difficult and often impossible.

Q. The firing line is essentially what?

A. Essentially the fighting part of the army; the other parts of the infantry are merely to repair its losses, protect its flanks, and reinforce it when necessary.

Q. Why and how are scouts used in the infantry attack?

A. Almost invariably the ground over which the attack advances is broken, and contains features that are either shelters or obstacles. Scouts are therefore sent out to the front to make a rapid reconnaissance and to signal information to the troops in rear. They are sent out usually as soon as the troops arrive within the zone of artillery fire, preceding the skirmishers by 150 yards, more or less, and uniting with the firing line when it comes to within 800 yards of the enemy.

Q. What is the two-fold object of the support?

A. To protect the flanks of the firing line, if on the flank of the general line, and to guard against the enemy breaking through any gaps that may exist in the firing line. These matters, though, are secondary, the paramount function of the support being to reinforce the firing line.

Q. By what considerations is the strength of the support affected?

A. Its strength depends on the degree of cover afforded by the ground over which the advance is made. Hence in open ground the support should be stronger than in ground offering shelter to the attack. At the beginning of the advance the support should be equal to at least one-half of the firing line; in general the two are of the same strength.

Q. What is usually the distance of the support from the firing line at the beginning of the attack?

A. About 200 yards. This distance is not invariable, being affected by circumstances of terrain and of fire. For example, it is greater on open ground than on ground affording shelter. No matter what the nature of the ground may be, the support should always be near enough to reinforce the firing line promptly; and, on the other hand, must, if possible, be far enough back to escape serious loss.

Q. How is the firing line reinforced from the support?

A. The best method is to send forward squads rather than single men, which should, as far as possible, fill the gaps of the firing line. But this method is not always practicable, and then the only thing to be done is to send forward individual men to find places as best they can.

Q. Why is the choice of the time to reinforce the firing line a matter of the greatest importance?

A. If delayed too long, the men will rush forward singly or in small squads, and the support will, without orders, melt away into the firing line. On the other hand, reinforcement should be delayed as long as possible, as the moral effect is greater in the later than in the earlier stages of the fight.

Q. State the general object of the reserve.

A. To guard the flanks and to reinforce the firing line.

Q. How should the reserve be formed, and where held relatively to the troops in front?

A. As long as possible, in column; and held in rear of the center or of the most exposed flank.

Q. What should be the distance of the reserve from the bodies of troops in front at the beginning of the attack, and how does this distance change as the attack progresses?

A. At the beginning of the attack the reserve should be from 500 to 700 yards from the firing line. As the attack proceeds this distance diminishes, for the firing line halts to fire, while the reserve advances uninterruptedly.

Q. How should the distance of the reserve from the firing line compare with that of the firing line from the enemy?

A. It should always be less; otherwise the enemy might overwhelm the firing line before the reserve could get up.

Q. How and when are reinforcements sent forward from the reserve?

A. Rarely by throwing the reserve bodily into the firing line, usually by feeding it steadily into the firing line when the latter is about 400 yards from the enemy. A portion is always held in hand for reinforcing just before the final assault.

Q. What should be the strength of the reserve as compared with the firing line and support, and what should the strength always be at the beginning of the fight?

A. Before it begins reinforcing, the reserve should be equal to the firing line and support combined. As a rule, it is equal to all in front of it, and at the opening of the combat, it should never be less than one-fourth of the entire first line.

Q. What are the objects of the second line?

A. To carry the first line with it in the final assault, should it be likely that a stubborn assault is to be encountered, to guard the flanks of the first line, and to renew the fight in case the first line is repulsed.

Q. What is the strength of the second line, its distance from the first, and under whose command should it be placed?

A. Its strength varies from one-third of the first to equality with it. At the beginning of the attack it should be 600 yards in rear of the first, and should be under the command of the officer in charge of the first line, so that the same mind that directs the attack may control the reinforcements at the critical moments.

Q. What are the duties of the third line?

A. The final assault must of course result in either success or failure. In the former case, the troops, disorganized by assault, are in no condition to meet a counter-charge by the enemy's reserves. It is to meet this counter-assault that the third line is specially intended. Moreover, the third line holds the captured position, which the assaulting troops may not always be able to do, and conducts the pursuit. In case of the repulse of the attack, the third line covers the re-formation or retreat of the defeated troops.

Q. Who commands the third line, what is its distance from the second, and what is its strength?

A. It is not necessarily under the command of the officer commanding the other two, but is generally under the immediate control of the commanding officer of the entire force composing the three lines. Its distance from the second at the beginning of the attack is about 600 yards, and its strength varies, being greater than that of the second and often equal to that of the first.

Q. What should be the formation of a regiment of infantry for the attack?

A. A regiment should be drawn up in two or three lines. The maximum front should not be greater than that of the regiment in one line in close order, increased by one-half the interval between adjacent regiments. If formed in two lines, the first line is composed of two battalions, the second of one; if formed in three lines, each is composed of one battalion, this being the formation generally adopted. In all cases the distance between the lines is 600 yards, more or less.

Q. Describe the steps taken in forming a regiment of infantry for attack.

A. Just before entering the first zone of artillery fire, the regiment (being in route formation) is formed front into line in three lines. The colonel directs the major commanding the first battalion to form for attack, and indicates the direction and object of the assault. The major at once designates the second and third companies for the fighting line, and the first and fourth for the reserve, and orders the attack formation to be taken. The captains of the companies designated for the fighting line each send forward a few scouts, under a non-commissioned officer, who is first instructed as to the direction and object of the movement. They also each designate each two sections for the firing line and two for the support, and when the scouts have advanced sufficiently, the companies are formed for attack, the firing line in close order, following the scouts at a distance of about 150 yards, the four sections of the support, each in line in close order, following the firing line at 200 yards distance, and the two companies of the reserve, in similar formation, following at a further distance of 300 yards. The support and the reserve are both so disposed as to protect the flanks of the firing line. The second line, in line of platoon columns with full intervals, follows the first at a distance of 600 yards, and the third line, in similar formation, follows the second at the same distance.

Q. When the firing line arrives at about 1400 yards from the enemy, what tactical formations are taken, what further changes are made as the attack advances?

A. At 1400 yards, the firing line forms lines of sections, and so does the support; at about 1200 yards, the firing line forms line of squads, the support remaining in line of sections. At 900 yards, the firing line deploys as skirmishers, the support forms lines of squads, and the reserve lines of sections.

Q. At what range does the firing line open fire, and what sort of fire should it use?

A. At 800 yards; volleys chiefly will be used, regulated by the section commanders. Each section halts to fire, and resumes the advance as soon as it

Attack Formation of a Regiment of Infantry
Firing Line about 3000 yds. from Hostile Position.

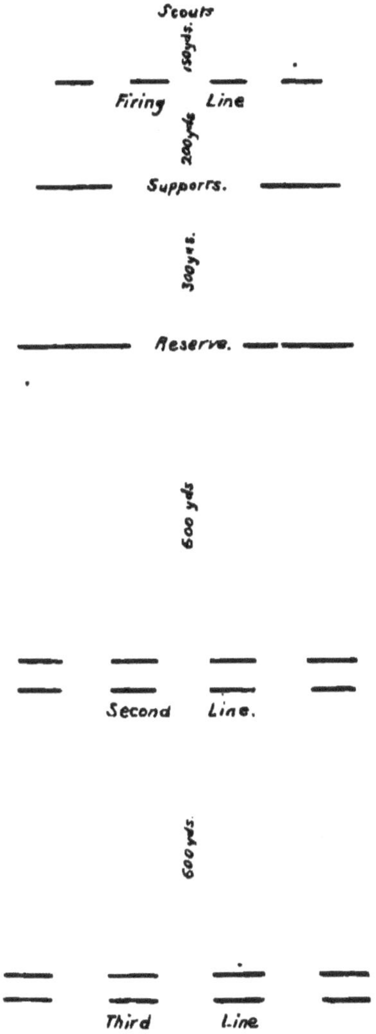

```
                Scouts
                  :
                 150yds.
    ___    ___    ___    .
         Firing    Line
                 200yds.
                  :
    ___         Supports.    ___    ___

                  :
                 300yds.
                  :

    ___         Reserve.    ___  ___

  .



                 600 yds



    ==    ==    ==    ==
         Second    Line.



                 600 yds



    ==    ==    ==    ==
          Third    Line
```

PLATE 1.

Attack Formation of Regiment of Infantry 900 yards from Hostile Position.

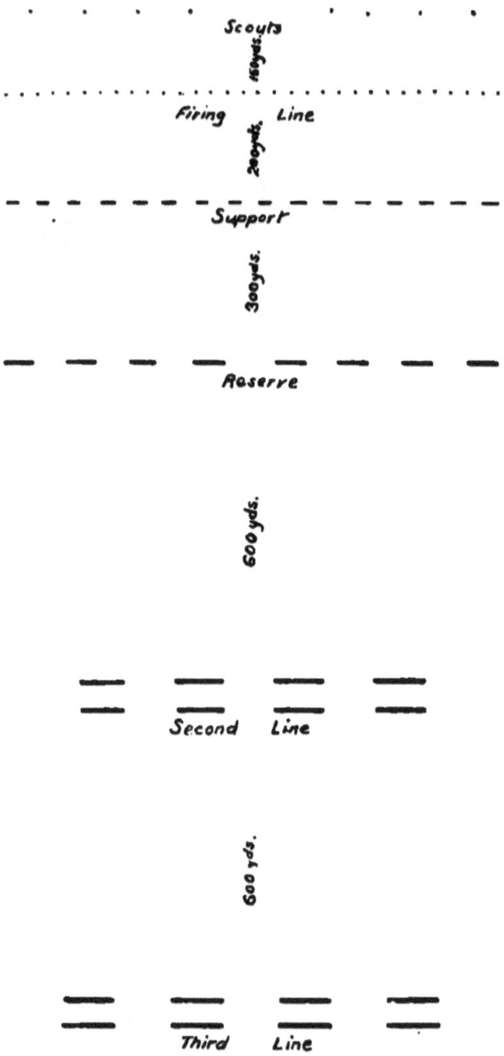

. . . .
Scouts

150 yds.

. . . .
Firing   Line

200 yds.

— —   — — — — — —   — — — —
Support

300 yds.

— —   — —   — —   — —   — —
Reserve

600 yds.

═   ═   ═   ═
Second   Line

600 yds.

═   ═   ═   ═
Third   Line

PLATE 2.

has fired the designated number of cartridges, the sections as nearly as possible halting and advancing together.

Q. At what point of the advance will rushes be found necessary.

A. At about 500 yards; moreover, the support will from now on be entirely absorbed in the firing line, its place being taken by the reserve. The second line will now form line of platoons, the third remaining unchanged.

Q. Describe the attack from this point.

A. The losses of the firing line being heavy, it clings to cover, and while holding its own, seems unable to advance. The battalion commander selects favorable ground from which to make the assault on the enemy's position, and throws the reserve forward into the firing line. The impetus thus given carries the firing line forward by rushes, and it succeeds in reaching a position about 200 yards in front of the enemy, where it kneels or lies down and opens rapid fire.

As soon as rapid fire is begun, the second line fixes bayonets and moves forward at double time. At a signal from the colonel given as the two lines unite, the trumpets sound the charge, and the men rush forward upon the enemy's position.

The third line hastens forward, occupies the captured position, pursues the retreating enemy, or defends the position from a counter-charge.

Q. Describe the formation of a brigade of infantry for the attack.

A. The brigade may be formed in one, two, or three lines, the best formation undoubtedly being

48   *Elements of Mililary Science.*

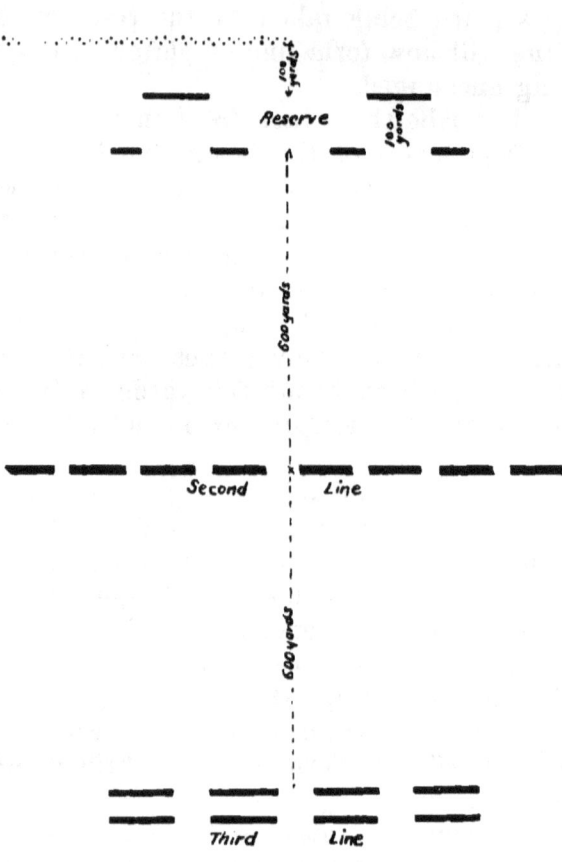

PLATE 3.

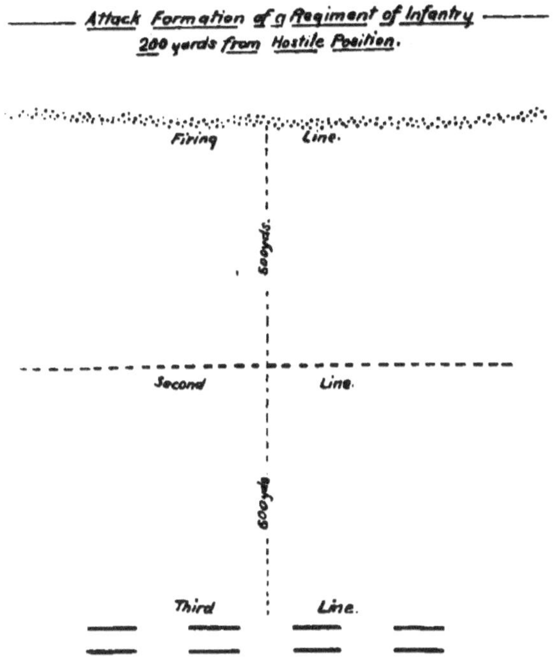

—— Attack Formation of a Regiment of Infantry ——
200 yards from Hostile Position.

··· Firing Line ···

500 yds.

— — — — — — — Second Line — — — — — — —

600 yds.

Third Line
═ ═ ═ ═

PLATE 4.

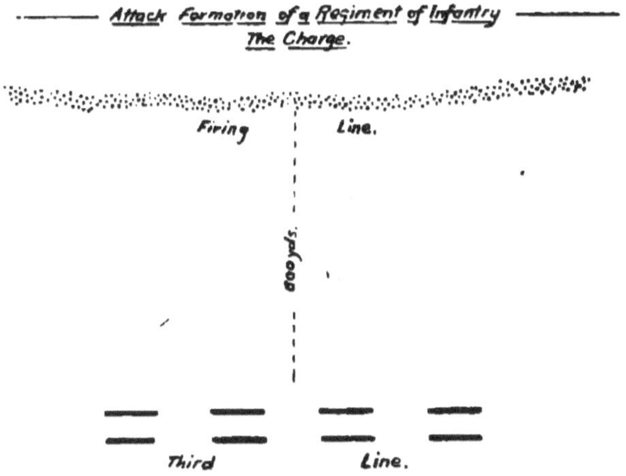

—— Attack Formation of a Regiment of Infantry ——
The Charge.

··· Firing Line ···

800 yds.

Third Line
═ ═ ═ ═

PLATE 5.

that of regiments side by side, each in three lines, a formation giving three battalions in each line.

Q. Give the general rules to be observed in conducting an infantry attack.

A. *(a)* Do not have a heavy firing line before coming within effective rifle range of the enemy; then employ in that line as many men as can use their rifles with the best effect.

(b) Regulate the fire from the beginning so that it may steadily increase in power up to the stage just preceding the final charge, when it should reach its maximum intensity.

(c) Guard carefully against an exhaustion of ammunition.

(d) Avoid a premature reinforcement of the firing line, in order that you may have men at hand to sustain it when the moral effect of reinforcement is greatest.

(e) Endeavor to prevent your men from being influenced by any panic or demoralization that may seize upon troops supported by them.

(f) Keep all your troops except the firing line in column until considerations of fire-action or protection from the enemy's fire demand deployment.

(g) Always endeavor to have in reserve a small body of formed troops for the moment when your attacking force is disordered by its own success or driven back in defeat; but do not keep large bodies out of action for this purpose.

Q. Give the three distinct phases of the infantry attack.

A. *(a)* The preparation, which consists of the reconnaissance of the terrain and of the hostile position, and of the use of artillery and long-range infantry fire to shake the enemy and prepare the way for the assault.

(b) The assault proper, which begins with the arrival of the infantry at effective ranges, and ends with the final charge on the enemy's position.

(c) The completion, which includes the occupation of the position by a formed body of troops (generally of the third line), and the re-formation of the victorious troops disordered by the assault. In case the assault fails, the third phase consists of the withdrawal of the attacking troops.

Q. What is a requisite for success in front attacks?

A. A great superiority in numbers and morale; for the increased range and power of fire-arms has made front attacks so costly that without this superiority they are all but certain to fail.

Q. What advantages are gained by a flank attack?

A. If the attack is of the nature of a surprise, the moral effect of flank fire is very great, and a small force may drive a much larger one from a position impregnable to assaults from the front.

Q. Why is a combination of front and of flank attacks necessary?

A. If a front attack alone is made, it is likely to fail; if a flank attack alone, the enemy can meet it by a change of front. A front attack is necessary, while the real or decisive attack is proceeding on the flank.

Q. In what two ways may a flank attack be made?

A. Either by extending the front so as to overlap

the enemy's line on one flank, and then wheeling in on the flank to be attacked, or by making a turning movement.

Q. Define a turning movement, and state what conditions are necessary to its success.

A. A turning movement is one made by detaching a force to make a *détour* and to fall on the enemy's flank. To be successful, it must be made out of the sight and beyond the range of the enemy.

Q. When should the troops for a flank attack be concentrated on the flank to be attacked?

A. This must generally be done after the enemy's attention is occupied by the front attack. The more earnestly the latter is pressed, the greater the likelihood of diverting the enemy's attention from the flank attack.

Q. What is the object of a force on the defensive, what are the conditions of a good defense, and how are these conditions best fulfilled?

A. The object of the defensive is to shatter the attack by its fire, so as to keep him from reaching the position at all, or if he does reach it, to force him to do so in so crippled a condition as to be easily overthrown by a counter-attack. Hence, an effective fire on the assailant and protection from his fire are essential conditions of a good defense; these conditions are best satisfied by utilizing natural or by making artificial cover, and by having a firing line of such density as to admit of the most effective use of the rifle by each man.

Q. What are the general characteristics of the defense?

A. The same as those of the attack. As in the

attack, so in the defense, the support is gradually fed into the firing line, and when short-range fire is admissible, the reserve pushed wholly or in part into the firing line. A second line is necessary, in case the first line of the defense is so crippled as to be unable to oppose the shock of the enemy.

Q. When and how should the defensive position be occupied by the firing line?

A. As the success of the attack depends largely on the assailant's knowledge of the position of the defense, the firing line should not be placed at once in full force upon the selected position. Usually the firing line takes up its position when the enemy is within 2000 yards. The line is ordinarily not of uniform strength at the probable points of attack; there should be as many men as can use the rifle with effect. Where obstacles exist, the force may be smaller.

Q. Why can long-range fire generally be used with more effect by the defense than by the attack?

A. Because ranges are more accurately known. Again, ammunition can be so much more easily supplied as to justify an expense of cartridges that would be impossible for the attack.

Q. What should be the objective of the defensive firing line?

A. The defensive firing line should direct its fire upon the nearest groups and echelons of attack, so as to impress the enemy that his own firing line is the most dangerous place into which he can put himself. If the enemy advance by alternate rushes, the portion of his force exposed in the forward rush should be the objective.

Q. What is the object of the support in the defensive?

A. In general, the same as in the attack. The position of the support cannot be definitely fixed; but, unless greatly exposed thereby, it should not be more than 75 to 100 yards from the firing line. In respect of strength, the support will often, though not necessarily, be equal in strength to the firing line. In some cases the support may be put into the firing line from the beginning of the combat.

Q. What is the position of the reserve in the defensive, and what is its strength?

A. The reserve should be centrally posted, under shelter if possible, at about 300 yards from the support. This distance, however, depends on the terrain. The strength of the reserve varies inversely with that of the firing line; a strong and well-sheltered firing line does not demand so strong a reserve as one that is weak and exposed.

Q. What are the functions of the second line?

A. To support the more exposed portions of the first line, to aid in local counter-attacks, and to protect the flanks. It is generally posted centrally, under shelter if possible, and at a distance from the first line dependent on the nature of the ground; this distance should not exceed 600 yards, and generally will be less.

Q. What are the functions of the third line?

A. Its chief function is to clinch the advantages due to the fire of the defense by a vigorous assumption of the offensive, and to assist the firing line by combining a flank attack with the heavy front fire delivered upon the enemy.

Q. What is the most important requisite of an infantry position?

A. A clear field of fire to the front and the flanks for a distance equal to the effective range of the rifle. The next consideration of importance is to secure adequate cover. Hence the ideal infantry defensive position is furnished by open ground sloping gently down to the enemy, with a free sweep of fire to the front.

Q. Why are hasty intrenchments used?

A. Because good natural cover can rarely be found. Hence troops on the defensive must furnish artificial cover by constructing intrenchments. These should be so traced as to allow effective frontal fire without exposure to enfilade. When constructed, they should be concealed as much as possible by covering the freshly turned earth with bushes, sod, etc., and if possible they should not be thrown up until the enemy has defined his attack. The embankment or parapet should be from 30 to 60 inches thick, whence the necessity of an efficient intrenching tool.

Q. Are hasty intrenchments ever of value on the offensive?

A. Yes; to fortify a position when captured, so as to hold it against a counter-attack.

Q. Compare the defensive with the offensive.

A. On the defensive, the position is chosen and the enemy may therefore be compelled to cross open ground under heavy fire. Fire discipline is more easily maintained, and ammunition more easily supplied. The line, too, is always more or less sheltered. The offensive enjoys the inestimable advantage of having a definite plan. It may deceive the enemy as to the real point of attack, thus compelling the defense to be strong at every point on which an attack may fall. It implies moral and numerical superiority. Finally, positive results can be obtained by the offensive and by the offensive only. Even the defensive must take the offensive if it would clinch its repulse of the attack by securing the advantage thus gained.

Q. How should ammunition be supplied on the battle-field?

A. An officer should be detailed in charge of the ammunition wagons of each regiment. These wagons formed into a regimental park should not be more than 1100 yards in rear of the firing line; they should indeed be pushed as far to the front as is possible without undue exposure. Each wagon when emptied should be sent back to the nearest ammunition column to be refilled, and its place should be taken by a full wagon without delay. Just before going into action, each man should be supplied with as much ammunition in addition to the amount usually carried as will fill his pockets and belts, and advantage should be taken of every lull or pause in the combat to replenish the supplies of the firing line.

Q. Has infantry anything to fear from cavalry?

A. Good infantry, if intact and plentifully supplied with ammunition, has, unless completely surprised, nothing to fear from cavalry. A line, if attacked, should halt and open fire; a skirmish line should rally by squads, and the support and reserve, if in column, should form line, the support guarding the flanks. If attacked in flank, the support and reserve should form on the threatened flank, the firing line rallying by groups or by sections.

Q. What is the effect of smokeless powder on infantry tactics?

A. The results of the employment of smokeless powder are as yet speculative. The absence of smoke will make better targets on both sides. The general opinion seems to be that the advantage flowing from the use of smokeless powder will lie chiefly with the defensive, whose line will now be scarcely visible, whereas formerly it was clearly defined by its own smoke. The assailant, on the other hand, will be constantly in plain view, and hence, besides thereby furnishing a better target, will necessarily disclose more or less plainly the objective of his attack.

CHAPTER IV.

CAVALRY IN ATTACK AND IN DEFENSE.

Q. How is a charge of cavalry made in line, why are a support and a reserve necessary, and where are they posted?

A. A charge in line is made in close order, boot to boot, the forward movement increasing in rapidity until it finally terminates in a shock delivered at full speed. The effect of the charge depends on the cohesion, weight, and speed of the charging force; the result, on the weapons of the trooper and on his skill in using them.

Whether successful or not, charging cavalry is always disordered by the shock; hence the necessity of a support to guard against a possible countercharge made on the disordered troopers. The support must be so posted as to attack the enemy's flank, or to protect that of its own attacking line. The position of the support is therefore on the flank exposed to the enemy, or from which it can best operate against the enemy. In general, the support should not be directly behind the attacking line, lest it be ridden down by the latter if defeated. As the support is usually drawn into the mellay, there must be a reserve to decide the victory or to ward off counter-attacks. The reserve is usually echeloned on the flank opposite to that of the support, unless this should be covered by natural obstacles, when it may be on the same side as the support. In general the idea is that in any case the support and reserve must relieve the attacking line of all apprehension in respect of its flanks.

Q. Of what parts should an attacking force of cavalry then be composed?

A. Of an attacking line containing about half the whole force; of a support, from one-fourth to one-third of the whole force; and of a reserve, from one-fourth to one-sixth.

Q. What should be the distance between the component parts of an attacking force of cavalry?

A. This distance varies with the strength of the attacking body. In the case of a troop, the support should be 80 yards from the attacking line, and the reserve not more than 150 from the support. For a brigade or a division, the former distance should be about 175, and the latter about 150—200 yards. The inner flank of the support should be from 50 to 75 yards beyond the outer or exposed flank of the attacking line, and the reserve should be similarly placed in respect of the inner or protected flank of the same line.

Q. At what pace should cavalry charge, and how is a charge conducted?

A. The advance should be made at a slow trot until the zone of effective artillery fire is reached, when the trot is increased to its limit and kept up until within 400 or 600 yards of the enemy. The column then deploys into line, and takes the gallop until within 75 or 50 yards of the enemy, when the charge is sounded and the horses are urged at full speed upon the enemy. When the attacking line charges, the support takes the full gallop, and when at the proper distance, charges against a flank or an intact organi-

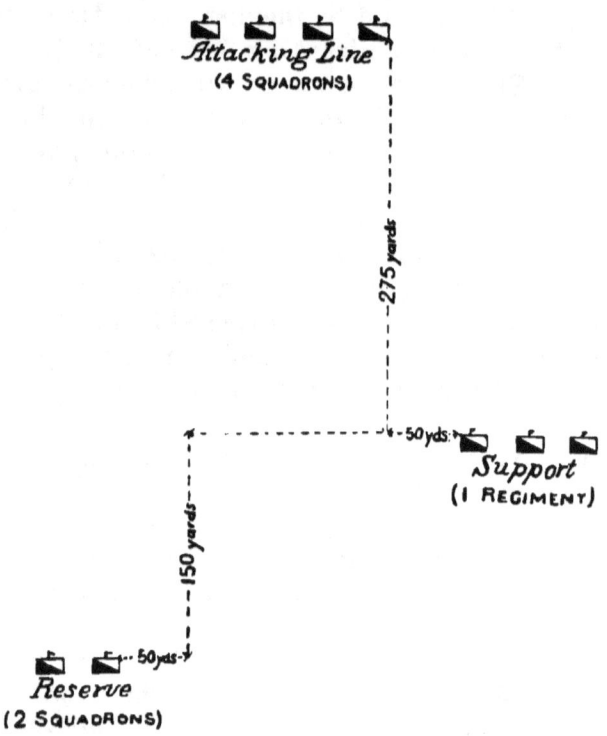

Plate 6.

zation of the enemy. The reserve is not habitually thrown into action except to meet an unexpected flank attack, or to take advantage of an opening to strike the enemy in flank.

If the charge succeeds, the enemy is pursued by the troopers engaged in the mellay until the pursuit can be taken up by the support and the reserve, when the attacking line re-forms, and itself acts as a support to the pursuing force. If the charge be unsuccessful, the attacking line should so withdraw as to avoid collision with the support and the reserve; these should both attack the pursuing force in flank.

Q. What sort of ground is best suited to a cavalry charge?

A. Undulating ground, if not broken by woods, enclosures, etc., as such ground affords considerable shelter without interfering with the force of the attack. A combination of open and inclosed ground is good, provided passages exist for passing from one open to another, and that open ground suitable for the charge is available immediately in front of the place of collision.

Q. Describe the use of ground scouts and of combat patrols.

A. A knowledge of the ground to be charged over is of great importance to the cavalry leader, as an obstacle seen too late may bring the charge to naught. Hence scouts are sent forward to reconnoiter the ground, communicating the results of their observations to the commander by signals. Combat patrols, consisting of two or three men each, are sent out to the flanks to give timely notice of threatened attacks by the enemy.

Q. What is the only sort of cavalry charge to give decisive results, and how are such charges made?

A. A charge on the enemy's flank. These may be made by causing a portion of the line to overlap the enemy, and to wheel inward, or by detaching a force to make a direct attack on the flank. The second case partakes of the nature of a surprise.

Q. Why is the moment when a cavalry charge should be made of importance?

A. If made too soon, the enemy will be found unshaken and unsurprised; if too late, the confusion, bad position, or other unfavorable circumstance of the enemy will be found remedied, and the opportunity will be lost. Hence the need of keen observation, quick decision, and firm resolution on the part of the cavalry commander.

Q. When cavalry charges in column, what should be the distance between subdivisions?

A. The distance should be such as to allow each to give timely support to the one in front, without being so close as to be compromised by its defeat. A charge in column of subdivisions gives a succession of shocks in the same place, and is therefore better than a charge in line, unless the latter includes a flank attack.

Q. How should the charge in column of fours be made?

A. Either from a close-order line or from an extended-order line, troopers using revolvers, and charging in couples with intervals of about six yards.

Q. Why will the number of cavalry battles be probably greater in the future than in the past?

A. The success of the campaign depends on the

proper performance of screening and reconnoitering duty, and this in turn depends on the superiority of one cavalry over the other. Hence each army will at the outset strive to overthrow the mounted force of its opponent, and, naturally, the attempt to break through the screen will lead to many mounted encounters. Further, during regular battles, the cavalry and the horse artillery will try to get on the flanks or rear of the enemy.

Lastly, almost every great battle will close with a cavalry battle between the covering and the pursuing cavalries.

Q. When are the best opportunities offered for an attack upon the enemy's cavalry?

A. When the enemy is issuing from a defile and presents a narrow front; when it can be surprised in column formation; when it can be taken in flank while charging another body, when exhausted; when it is changing formation or else is on ground unfavorable to its deployment.

Q. By what bodies will the combats of cavalry with cavalry generally be fought?

A. By the cavalry divisions, as the corps cavalry will be used in conjunction with the other troops of the corps.

Q. State the different circumstances under which cavalry may be used with effect in charging infantry.

A. *(a)* When the infantry is demoralized or of poor quality.

(b) When the infantry can be taken by surprise.

(c) When the infantry is out of ammunition.

(d) When the infantry is broken by the fire of the opposing infantry or artillery.

(e) When the infantry is engaged with the opposing infantry.

(f) To compel the infantry to take up such a formation as to present a good target to the fire of the opposing infantry or artillery.

(g) To check an attack of the enemy's infantry and gain time for the arrival of reinforcements.

(h) When the infantry is exhausted by a prolonged contest with the hostile infantry.

(i) When the infantry is disordered in retreat.

(j) In covering a retreat.

(k) To cut through a surrounding force of hostile infantry.

Q. What is the effect on infantry of a threatened attack by cavalry?

A. Cavalry may thus sometimes check the advance or attack of infantry.

Q. How should cavalry be formed to attack infantry?

A. The formation of cavalry for this purpose depends on that of the infantry itself. Against infantry in masses or in line in close order, line of columns or successive lines at about 200 yards distance should be used. When the infantry is in extended order, it should be charged by foragers, supported by about half the force in close order. In charging infantry, cavalry should take the shortest line and endeavor to take the infantry in flank. In any case, cavalry should be careful not to mask the fire of its own infantry and artillery.

Q. State the three general cases in which artillery may be attacked by cavalry.

A. *(a)* When artillery, hurried into action, is unsupported by other arms.

(b) When the infantry supports have been driven back, or have exhausted their ammunition, and the artillery stands alone.

(c) When artillery can be surprised, especially while limbering or unlimbering.

Q. How should cavalry be formed for the attack of artillery?

A. In attacking a battery, the cavalry forms in two or three parts; the attacking line charges as foragers, divides near the center as it approaches, and assaults the battery on both flanks. The support advances and secures the battery; the reserve follows in close order to meet a counter-attack, if made. A battery captured should be carried off, but if this be impossible, the guns should be disabled.

Q. Enumerate the purposes for which dismounted fire-action may be usefully employed.

A. *(a)* To drive away or capture small bodies of infantry or partisan troops, who endeavor to check the progress of raiding or reconnoitering cavalry.

(b) To force a defile which blocks an advance, and thus avoid a delay.

(c) To seize and hold localities until the arrival of the infantry.

(d) To reinforce infantry in emergencies.

(e) To fill up a gap in the line of battle.

(f) In an enclosed, wooded, or broken country, where mounted action is impracticable.

(g) In covering a retreat.

(h) When exhausted or defeated cavalry is called upon to resist a charge of fresh cavalry.

(i) In conjunction with cavalry mounted.

(j) Whenever cavalry, through force of circum-

stances, is deprived of the power of using mounted action.

Q. How are dismounted men maneuvered and fought?

A. In essentially the same manner as infantry, with a skirmish line, support, and reserve, except that a mounted reserve is kept for emergencies. On the offensive the men should get up, as close as possible before dismounting; at least, they should get up to the zone of effective artillery fire. The position captured, the mounted reserve pursues the enemy. When dismounted cavalry is on the defensive, all the reserve should be put in the firing line, as soon as the enemy's attack is developed. If the attack be by a superior force, the action should be discontinued in sufficient time to allow the defender to retire and mount.

Q. Of what value is dismounted fire-action to cavalry?

A. It adds immeasurably to the independence and fighting power of cavalry; but it is only the complement of mounted action, and must not be regarded as the chief use of cavalry.

Q. When may mounted fire-action be used?

A. *(a)* As a means of temporary resistance by small scouting parties, or by the point and flankers of an advance guard.

(b) In the pursuit of a beaten enemy, when a mounted charge is impracticable.

(c) In covering a retreat when the pursuit is so active and so strong as to make it unsafe to dismount and inexpedient to charge.

(d) When the opposing cavalry is charging over heavy and unfavorable ground.

Q. What are the objects for which cavalry raids are undertaken?

A. *(a)* To threaten or to destroy the communications of the enemy, thus compelling him to weaken himself for their protection, or delay his advance.

(b) To check an invading army by operations against its communications and the capture of its immediate base of supplies.

(c) To make a diversion in favor of the main army by drawing off troops in pursuit of the raiding force.

(d) To gain information.

(e) To cause alarm in the enemy's country, and thus destroy confidence in the enemy's commanding general, or create a sentiment unfavorable to the prosecution of the war.

(f) To interfere with the mobilization and concentration of the enemy's forces at the beginning of a campaign.

(g) To devastate the enemy's country and destroy his resources.

(h) To effect the release of prisoners.

Q. When are raids practicable, and why should they never be undertaken without an important object?

A. Raids are rarely practicable in the enemy's country on account of the hostility of the population. As they wear out the horses, impose great fatigue upon the men, and tend to demoralize them by breeding a spirit of depredation, so they should not be undertaken unless the object justifies all the risks involved. Among these not the least is that of being absent from the army when a decisive battle is to be fought.

Q. Describe the composition and preparation of a raiding force.

A. A raiding force should be composed of well-mounted, well-disciplined, self-reliant troops, complete organizations being used instead of detachments from various ones, and should usually vary in number from 1000 to 3000 men. For quick work, requiring secrecy, small bodies are best; for devastating a large region and destroying resources, a large force may be used. As a rule, no infantry should form a part of a raiding force; mountain artillery may frequently be used to great advantage, in the proportion of two guns to a 1000 men. If not available, then horse artillery may be employed. A raiding force should live on the country, but rations for a few days ought to be carried for emergencies. Each trooper might be required to carry as many as five days' rations on his person, and always 200 rounds of ammunition and a pair of spare horseshoes. The objective of the raid should in all cases be clearly determined in advance, and the commander should be a man competent to attain it.

Q. What constructions should a raiding force seek to destroy?

A. Bridges, railways, rolling stock, tunnels, telegraph lines, etc.

Q. How does the tactics of cavalry compare with that of any other arm?

A. It is more varied than that of any other arm. It embraces shock-action in line and in column; fire-action mounted and on foot; a combination of fire- and shock-action either mounted or dismounted; and the simultaneous use of fire-action, dismounted and shock-action mounted by different parts of the same command. The arms, training, and tactical formations of modern cavalry adapt it to use on varied ground, and in every phase of the battle, and sustain General Kilpatrick's apothegm, that "cavalry can fight anywhere except at sea."

CHAPTER V.

Artillery in Attack and in Defense.

Q. Why is artillery indispensable to an attack?

A. First, to oppose the guns of the defense, so that the infantry may take up at comparative leisure a suitable formation for attack.

Second, to protect the infantry during the attack, from the fire of the opposing batteries, by delivering such a fire upon these as to compel them to turn their attention from the foot troops to the assailant's guns.

Q. What further use is made of artillery in the attack?

A. The defender's batteries are scarcely ever permanently silenced; it follows, therefore, as the attack proceeds, that the assailing infantry will still have to meet the fire of hostile guns. It is upon these that the guns of the attack bestow their attention, in order to crush them, if possible, before the assailants reach the position, and in any case to make it possible to reach effective rifle range without undue loss. As the attack gets closer and closer to the enemy, the artillery fires over the heads of the assailants as long as it may do so without injury to its own side.

Q. Of what value is artillery in the case of a repulse? in the case of a success?

A. In the case of a repulse, it forms a solid support on which the infantry can re-form; in the case of a success, the batteries are pushed forward to the captured position in order to check any counter-attack.

Q. How does the tactics of artillery compare with that of the other arms?

A. It is far simpler, for artillery always fights in line; the advance in column of route, and the deployments therefrom, with the advance in line, comprise all essential maneuvers. In action, the interval between guns should never be less than 10 yards, as a lesser interval makes the battery too good a target, nor more than 40, as a greater interval would put the guns out of the direct control of the battery commander.

Q. What are the requisites of a good artillery position?

A. As artillery can act only by the efficiency of its fire, a good position should furnish a clear range to the front and flanks as far as the limit of effective fire. The general position should be at right angles to the line of fire, and should have enough room not only for the guns to be immediately placed in position, but also for the others to be brought up later. There should be easy communication to the front and rear, and no cover for hostile infantry skirmishers within 1000 yards of the line of guns anywhere in front. The flanks should be carefully protected, as these are the specially weak points of an artillery line. The *indispensable* condition to be satisfied by any position is freedom of movement to the front.

Q. Describe briefly the successive positions to be occupied by artillery in the attack.

A. The first position occupied is called the reconnoitering position, and is about 3000 yards from the enemy. It should, if possible, be occupied unseen by the enemy until fire is opened. Such a position may sometimes be found on the outer edge of the first zone. In general, the position selected should be as near the enemy as possible, so long as there is little or no danger of an attack by the hostile infantry too severe to be repelled by the guns or their escort.

From the reconnoitering position, fire is opened on the enemy, under the protection of which the infantry deploys and the commander makes his plan of attack. Every attempt is made by the artillery of each side to overwhelm that of the other, and hence the artillery duel begins in this position.

The second position is called the "duel" position, and is 2000 yards, more or less, from the enemy. This position is assumed as soon as the supporting infantry can be pushed up; it is from this position that the main fire is kept up against the hostile batteries.

The third position is the supporting position; it is about 1000 yards from the enemy and derives its name from the fact that the guns now directly support the infantry attack proper. It should be carefully borne in mind that all the distances mentioned are subject to variations depending on the circumstances of each separate case.

Q. How is the battery subdivided for combat purposes?

A. Into, first, the "fighting battery" or first line, composed of all the guns and of 3 caissons; second, the reserve, comprising the remaining caissons, 6 in number, spare horses, and as many of the spare men as can be accommodated on the caissons and spare horses for rapid movements; and third, the train, made up of the remaining spare men, of the battery wagon and forage, and store wagon.

The reserve and train feed the fighting battery during the combat.

Q. Should the artillery fire over the heads of the infantry of its own side?

A. Not if it can be helped, but sometimes this measure is necessary.

Q. Of what does the fire tactics of artillery consist?

A. Of the art of hitting the enemy. It is requisite, therefore, in order to obtain the enormous effect of which this arm is capable, that it have a definite objective upon which to direct its fire. Hence, as a general rule, "the fire of artillery is directed against that arm of the enemy which at the time is predominant, or which is capable of inflicting the greatest loss on the infantry or cavalry that the artillery is supporting." (United States Light Artillery Drill Regulations.)

Q. How is artillery fire classed in respect of rate?

A. As slow, ordinary, and rapid. In slow fire there is no specified interval of time between the firing of the guns, all being fired in succession by the command of the battery commander. The rate of slow fire is variable, but is generally from 30 seconds to 1 minute for each shot. Ordinary fire is at the rate of from 15 to 20 seconds between discharges, and is the fire habitually used. Rapid fire is at the rate of 7 seconds to the round. It is used against artillery in movement; by one echelon of artillery in covering the advance of another; when the decisive infantry attack is about to take place; to repel infantry at close range; and, generally, when the opportunity for an effective fire is very fleeting or when the target presented is very favorable,

Q. What is the great objective of the artillery of both the defense and the attack?

A. To shatter the opposing infantry. This requires that the opposing artillery should first be overmastered; if the assailing batteries succeed in doing this, the success of the infantry attack is generally assured; if not, this attack will probably fail. Hence, during the artillery duel (3000—2000 yards), every attempt should be made to crush the opposing artillery. The decisive engagement of the opposing guns being at about 2000 yards, it follows that at this range the utmost endeavor should be made, while not neglecting the whole line of guns, to concentrate an overwhelming fire on each part in turn. The special object sought should be the destruction of the *personnel*, as the damage to the *matériel* is generally trifling.

Q. Why is the artillery preparation of the infantry attack more important to-day than formerly?

A. Because infantry on the defensive is now generally sheltered by hasty intrenchments, and because the range and destructive effect of its weapons expose the assailant to more severe and long-continued fire than was formerly the case.

Q. After silencing the enemy's guns, or at least establishing a marked superiority over them, what should the artillery of the attack do?

A. It should direct a heavy fire upon the point of attack.

Q. Describe the manner of supporting the infantry attack by artillery.

A. As soon as the order is given to the infantry to advance, all the guns turn their fire on the point of attack, for the hostile infantry is now the objective and the part of the enemy capable of inflicting the most serious loss on the assailant. A part of the guns push on with the infantry, regarding nothing but the support of the latter at close quarters; these guns deliver a fire at close range, endeavoring to shatter the reserves, to overwhelm any fresh batteries the enemy may try to bring up, etc.

Q. How long should the artillery keep up its fire in the support of the infantry attack?

A. Long enough to keep the hostile infantry from returning to its position and presenting a good front to the assault; but not so long as to fire into its own infantry as the latter gets closer and closer to the enemy. A safe rule is to keep up the fire on the enemy's main position until the final charge, and then to throw shrapnel far enough back to reach the enemy's reserves.

Q. When the hostile position is carried, what should the artillery do?

A. It should hasten forward to assist in a further advance, or to check a counter-attack. If the infantry attack fail, the advancing batteries halt, and come into action in order to cover the withdrawal of the infantry.

Q. In what way does artillery give solidity to attack formation?

A. By furnishing points of support to large bodies of infantry in extended order that are of great value in the tumult and danger of battle.

Q. What is the first objective of the artillery of the defense?

A. To open the most effective fire possible on the batteries of the attack, for if it can gain the superiority over the latter, the infantry attack will probably not be made. If, however, the attacking batteries gain the upper hand, then the guns of the defense are turned on the advancing troops, and keep up this fire until either the attack is repulsed or until the position is abandoned. In the former case the guns must assist in the counter-attack; in the latter, they must cover the retreat of the infantry.

Q. What are the characteristics of a good position for artillery on the defensive?

A. They are essentially those of a good position for attack, as the object in each case is to *hit*. Hence there must be a clear view to the front and to the flanks. As the flanks are the essentially weak points of the defense, they must be supplied with guns, so that if the enemy attempt a turning movement, he will be compelled to deploy at a distance, and thus give the defense time to prepare to meet this attack. Some of the guns should from the first be posted so as to cover weak points, and others so as to compel a deployment at a distance; but the greater part should not be placed in position until the attack is more or less developed, so as not to unmask the position. Hence the batteries should be brought up near the position, and held under cover until the proper moment for putting them into action.

Q. Discuss briefly the question of cover for guns.

A. Natural cover should be used if possible, and, if there is time, gun-pits made. Screening the guns will often be easier than getting actual cover; the effect of screening is to deceive the enemy as to the range, and thus lead him to waste his ammunition. Artificial cover should be concealed as much as possible by brushwood, turf, etc. Cover for the *personnel* is more important than cover for the *matériel;* the men should be sheltered first and then the horses.

Q. What is the position of the artillery relative to the infantry in the defense?

A. In the opening stages of the combat, the artillery is the more important arm. Hence the most important points are held by it, a few guns being run up and the rest held in readiness to come forward when needed. Small parties of infantry and of cavalry are pushed forward to baffle reconnoitering parties. As the battle proceeds, these are called in, but skirmishers are kept about 500 yards to the front, whose business it is to keep the hostile skirmishers back 500 yards more, and thus relieve the guns of all anxieties on this score.

Q. What is the objective of the batteries of the defense?

A. As in the attack, the assailing artillery is the chief target in the first zone, and his infantry in the second and the third.

Q. What are the duties of the batteries of the defense during the artillery duel?

A. To overwhelm, if possible, the guns of the attack. But cases may arise in which this is of secondary importance, as, after all, the crushing of the enemy's infantry is the final objective. Hence, if the position is so strong that the hostile artillery can do it no harm, or if the batteries of the defense are relatively weak, or if the hostile infantry is compelled to deploy at very long range, the duel should be declined, and the guns kept under cover until the decisive infantry attack is made.

Q. When the hostile infantry is engaged, what are the duties of the artillery of the defense?

A. It should apply itself exclusively to the assaulting columns, regardless of the hostile guns. For if the infantry is not checked, any damage to the enemy's guns will be of no value in deciding the action, while if it is checked, his guns may be safely ignored.

Q. How should guns be withdrawn from action?

A. When the enemy's artillery has such an ascendency as to compel withdrawal from action, or when it is necessary to fall back on a second position, the batteries should withdraw deliberately at a walk, only a part of the batteries retiring at once. These take up a position on the rallying position in rear and cover by their fire the withdrawal of the remaining batteries. To retire in good order, dispositions must be made in advance, before the enemy's infantry has come up to the attack. But if the attack has been begun, the batteries must remain on the line, and, if necessary, sacrifice itself: it is no disgrace to lose guns gallantly fought to the bitter end.

Q. What may be said of the ability of artillery to defend its own front against infantry and cavalry?

A. In open ground it may be asserted confidently that artillery can defend its own front from attacks of infantry. But it may be equally confidently asserted that artillery alone cannot by its fire drive a resolute enemy from his line of defense. Cavalry, even more easily than infantry, can be repelled by artillery fire on open ground. But an unexpected attack by cavalry on the flank or rear of artillery, or while the latter is limbering or unlimbering, would be disastrous.

Q. Upon what does a battery depend for ammunition?

A. First, on its own limbers and caissons; next on the ammunition columns; and lastly, on the ordnance trains. The limbers, during an action, are kept on the flank of their batteries; the caissons of the fighting batteries, each in rear of its own platoon. The ammunition columns should approach more or less closely to the line of battle as long as the action is progressing favorably; in the opposite case, they should remain at a distance, except such caissons as are absolutely necessary to keep the guns supplied. During an action, no opportunity should be lost to replenish the ammunition of the batteries, limbers and caissons being refilled to their utmost capacity whenever possible, as, for example, during lulls in the combat.

Q. What are the functions of horse artillery?

A. The distinctive characteristic of horse artillery is its mobility. Hence it is particularly valuable as a part of the corps artillery, because it can be so quickly moved where needed, and also valuable as an auxiliary of cavalry in attack and defense. As part of the corps artillery, it is used to extend the line of battle, to support flank attacks, to reinforce threatened points, and in general for any operation involving the rapid entry of guns into action.

It is, however, with cavalry that horse artillery finds its greatest use. It supports this arm by its fire-action, and prepares the way for its charges, much as field artillery prepares the way for infantry. This similarity is all the more marked when cavalry fights on foot. In pursuit, or in covering a retreat, horse artillery is invaluable.

Q. How may horse artillery be used in reconnaissance? in a regular battle?

A. In reconnaissance, to drive in outposts and to develop the hostile position. In the preliminary phases of battle, to develop the enemy's position, and to force the hostile infantry columns to deploy prematurely. It is, moreover, very efficacious in the cavalry engagements that so frequently mark the beginning and the close of a great battle.

Q. What is the objective of the fire of the horse artillery of a cavalry division?

A. It should, if possible, be the hostile cavalry; but if this is not in sight, then the hostile artillery. As the hostile cavalry moves to the attack, its first line should be crushed, if possible; then its support and reserve. If the enemy's artillery should get the upper hand of our own cavalry, then part of the horse artillery should return the hostile fire, but it must not be forgotten that the principal target should always be the enemy's cavalry.

Q. What should be done with horse artillery in a general engagement?

A. If the cavalry is guarding the flanks, the horse artillery remains with it, for it may be needed; but if the cavalry is in reserve, then the horse batteries reinforce the general artillery line. In case of victory, the horse artillery accompanies the pursuit.

Q. What, probably, will be the influence of smokeless powder on artillery tactics?

A. As the firing line will now be scarcely visible, it can not be so easily distinguished by artillery as in the days when it defined itself by its own smoke. Hence, there is greater need than ever for artillery to accompany infantry in attack. The smoke no longer marking the position of the guns, artillery can remain in action longer than formerly; but, on the other hand, the absence of smoke in itself makes the battery more conspicuous, if it can be seen at all. Fire will hereafter be more continuous, as a battery will no longer be inconvenienced by its own smoke.

Q. Give the general principles governing the employment of artillery in battle.

A. I. Artillery should be brought into action at the very beginning of the battle, and should be actively employed as long as an enemy remains on the field.

II. It should be employed in masses, and should concentrate its fire; but it must be remembered that massing guns does not consist in posting the batteries contiguously, but in keeping them together under unity of command, so as to admit of mutual support and of the direction of their fire on a common objective.

III. It should take up a position as close to the enemy as it can without incurring unnecessary and ruinous losses.

IV. It should not feel called upon to blaze away the moment it comes into position, but it should endeavor to open an *effective* fire with the least possible delay.

V. It must never be forgotten that the value of artillery depends upon the accuracy of its fire.

VI. Artillery should always fire at a definite object, and should avoid "shelling" the woods, or engaging in any other ineffective cannonade.

VII. Every opportunity should be taken to replenish ammunition. The supply must not be allowed to fail, especially at critical moments.

VIII. The principal task of the artillery is to crush the enemy's infantry. It turns its attention to his artillery only as a means of getting rid of an obstacle to its attempts upon his infantry, or as a means of protecting its own infantry from the fire of the enemy's guns. In a cavalry battle, the cavalry is the objective of the artillery fire.

IX. When the attack is successful, the artillery must push forward to secure the captured position.

X. In case of defeat, the artillery must be prepared to cover the retreat, and, if necessary, to sacrifice itself for the safety of the rest of the army.

XI. It should never abandon a position unless ordered to do so. The loss of guns is highly honorable when, by remaining in action until the last moment, they have inflicted serious loss upon the enemy.

CHAPTER VI.

THE THREE ARMS COMBINED.

Q. What is meant by the term "plan of battle"?

A. When an army comes in contact with the enemy, and the strategical operations are about to culminate in a tactical decision, its commander must first decide whether to attack or to stand on the defensive. If the decision be in favor of the offensive, he must next determine whether to attack the enemy in front, to combine front and flank attacks, or to attempt to pierce some point of the hostile line. Having settled upon the method of attack, he must next decide upon the points of the opposing line upon which the attack should fall. These matters determined, he must provide for the combination of the several arms so as to obtain their most efficient mutual support and concentrated action, and make the best use of the terrain. These decisions and arrangements constitute the plan of battle.

Q. How is the question of the defensive or of the offensive usually decided?

A. Generally by circumstances as they develop. The choice sometimes lies in the commanding officer, who must then carefully weigh all questions of terrain, morale, relative numbers, characteristics of the enemy, etc.

Q. Why, as a rule, should a frontal attack not be made?

A. Because it is the least decisive mode of assailing the enemy. If successful, it merely drives him back on his base, thus resulting in a barren victory. It may, however, be necessary; for example, when the enemy's flanks rest on impassable objects. To be successful, it must in any case be made with a force larger than the enemy's.

Q. Why are flank attacks necessary, and with what are they usually combined?

A. Since frontal attacks are rarely decisive and generally impracticable, some other mode of overthrowing the enemy must be sought, and the one generally adopted is the combination of front and of flank. The necessity is this combination has already been mentioned.*

Q. Why should a simultaneous attack on both flanks be avoided?

A. Because ordinarily this would so weaken the center as to expose it dangerously to counter-attack.

Q. What is the effect of piercing the enemy's front?

A. An attack piercing the enemy's front is more decisive than any other, for it generally results in cutting off a part of the hostile army from its base, and causing either surrender or annihilation. Such a method of attack is, however, rarely practiced to-day.

Q. What is meant by the "order of battle"?

A. The relative tactical positions of the opposing forces in preparation for battle, or during the encounter.

Q. What are the three orders of battle, and how does each come into existence?

A. First, the parallel, when the attack is made

---

*See page 51.

along the whole line; then, the concave, when an attempt is made to turn both flanks of the enemy; lastly, the convex, when the attempt is made to pierce the front.

Q. State the advantages and the disadvantages of the various orders of battle.

A. The parallel rarely yields decisive results, and is not adopted except from necessity. The concave order opposes a converging to a diverging fire, but, unless it completely encloses the enemy, one or both flanks are dangerously exposed to counter-attack; if, however, too great an expansion is made, the center is liable to be pierced by the enemy. The concave is usually preferable to the convex order, and indeed some variety of the concave order is usually chosen. Sometimes the convex disposition is forced on a commanding general by the necessities of the case, as in the passage of a river, when troops are pushed forward to cover the passage, and the other troops afterward take position on the flanks of these. In the convex order the fire of the troops is divergent, and the enemy's fire on one wing may take the other in reverse; if the center of the line is pierced, both wings are taken in flank.

In general, any offensive plan is faulty that does not contemplate the turning of a flank.

Q. How is the choice of the point of attack determined?

A. By tactical considerations, if the sole object of the attack is to gain a victory and the possession of the field; by strategical considerations, if the object is to gain the greatest results from the battle. For examples of strategical considerations, if an army is connected by one flank with its base, attack that flank, so as to cut the enemy from his base, and therefore from supports and succor. Or, if an army is connected by its flank with a fort, attack that flank; if the line of retreat lies obliquely in rear of one wing, that wing should be the point of attack, for, in case of success, the enemy is cut off from his line of retreat.

Q. Give some examples of tactical considerations in choosing the point of attack.

A. The enemy's advanced posts should be captured, unless so far apart that the attack can be made between them. If the advanced posts are strong and close together, they must be captured. If a strongly fortified position lies in the line of battle, the attack should bear on points more easily carried, and from which the fortified post or position can be assailed in rear. When one of the hostile flanks rests on an impassable obstacle, the other extremity of the wing so situated forms a tempting point of attack, for, if the front is pierced, the troops so cut off may be thrown back on the obstacle, and either destroyed or captured.

Q. Give reasons why a reserve should always be provided.

A. A reserve is necessary to give a vigorous blow at a timely moment, either to clinch a success or to check an advantage gained by the enemy. This reserve varies in strength; it may often be one-fourth of the whole; it must always be used at exactly the right moment. If put in too soon, it will not be available for the moment of exhaustion found in every battle when the victory will go to that combatant who first can resume the offensive; if put in too late, there may

be nothing left for it but to cover the retreat that
might have been prevented by its timely use.

Q. State the functions of each arm in combination with the others.

A. The infantry protects and supports the artillery; the artillery prepares the way for the infantry, supports it in the attack, and protects it in the retreat. The cavalry must reconnoiter the enemy, protect the flanks of the army, support and gain time for the other arms by vigorous charges when they are sorely pressed, and reap the fruits of victory by an energetic pursuit.

Q. Into what three parts may an attack be divided?

A. Into the preparation, the attack proper, and the occupation of the position or the withdrawal from action.

Q. Describe the preparation for the attack.

A. The preparation for the attack is made by the advance guard. Meeting the enemy, it endeavors to drive him back until it encounters serious resistance, when it continues to fight a delaying action until the arrival of reinforcements. The artillery is the first to come up; it occupies the reconnoitering position, tries to develop the enemy by drawing the fire of his batteries, and begins the duel with his artillery. The proportion of infantry engaged so far is small, being mainly employed as skirmishers in front of the artillery, or else held in compact bodies on the flanks. During these operations the main body of the infantry is approaching, and takes position as the hostile position is developed, and while the commanding general is maturing his plan. As soon as the dispositions of the infantry are completed, the artillery moves forward and begins the duel. All the guns should now be put in, and deliver as effective a fire as possible on the enemy's line. During the duel, the infantry completes its preparations for the attack, and is moving forward to effective rifle-range of the enemy. The termination of the artillery duel marks the end of the preparatory stage, and the infantry passes on to the real attack.

Q. Describe the attack proper.

A. The infantry of the first line is now within 800—1000 yards from the enemy, and directs its attack on points battered by the preceding artillery fire. The assault is made as already described. The artillery concentrates its fire on the points of attack, the divisional batteries advancing to the supporting position and pouring a heavy fire on the hostile infantry.

During the attack the cavalry on the flanks seeks opportunities to charge, and especially guards the advancing infantry from all attacks by the hostile cavalry. A portion of the reserve is ordered up to support and to revive a flagging attack, or to check a counter-stroke by the enemy. The attack culminates in the merging of the entire first line in the firing line; rapid magazine fire is opened and the line throws itself upon the enemy with the bayonet. The second line usually joins in the charge, the artillery firing shrapnel as long as it can do so without injury to its own side.

Q. What are the special points to be considered in preparing and carrying out an attack by a force of all three arms?

I. The clearest possible understanding of the nature and extent of the enemy's position.

II. A definite object to be gained by the attack.

III. A careful selection of the points of attack, and the formation of a plan of battle, which should not be changed unless circumstances absolutely compel an alteration therein.

IV. The concentration of a powerful artillery fire on the point selected for attack.

V. False attacks on other points, to prevent the enemy from divining the real objective of the attack.

VI. The support of the infantry by artillery, both in the duel and in the supporting positions.

VII. Prompt use of the reserves at the decisive moment.

VIII. Keeping a force of cavalry well in hand to guard the flanks, follow up a success, cover a defeat, or make a diversion.

Q. Describe the occupation of the hostile position after a successful assault.

A. After a successful assault, the first and second lines are generally disorganized. Hence the third line pushes forward to hold the captured position, and to furnish cover behind which the first and second lines can re-form. The cavalry and the horse artillery should pursue, followed as soon as possible by the first and the second lines and the field batteries.

Q. In the case of a repulse, how should the withdrawal be made?

A. The infantry endeavors to withdraw by alternate bodies, the withdrawing body being covered by the fire of the rest. The principal protection must be offered by the artillery and the cavalry, each of which must sacrifice itself if necessary.

Q. In taking up the defensive, what three advantages should the commanding officer endeavor to secure?

A. He should endeavor to select a position that will guard his line of retreat, facilitate the tactical coöperation of the three arms, and enable him at the opportune moment to pass from the defensive to the offensive. The first and the second conditions are important; the third may be ignored in a purely defensive battle.

Q. What should be the character of the ground in front of the position?

A. It should be open, so as to afford a clear field of fire and such an unobstructed view that the enemy cannot approach anywhere within range unseen.

Q. How should the terrain in front of the position be prepared, if time permit?

A. It should be covered with military obstacles, such as abatis, pits, wire entanglements, etc. Fences and hedges may often be utilized to great advantage.

Q. What is one of the first requirements of the defensive position proper—*i. e.*, the line on which the men are stationed?

A. It should be suited in extent to the size of the force to occupy it. If too wide in extent, it will be weakly occupied; if the extent be too small, the men will be so crowded as to be incapable of efficient action, and besides will suffer unnecessary loss. Seven men per yard, including reserves, may be regarded as ample for the defense of a position.

Q. Mention another essential of a good defensive position.

A. Good cover. Natural cover for the reserves may often be found, but protection for troops in action must generally be provided by intrenchments. These enable a commanding officer to hold a part of his line with a comparatively light force, while massing greater numbers elsewhere for offensive movements. Intrenchments should never be constructed so as to be an obstacle to the advance of the defensive troops, when it is decided to make a counter-stroke. As a rule, it is better to have the troops make their own intrenchments.

Q. How should the flanks of a defensive position be protected?

A. By resting them on strong points, either natural or artificial. An example is a hill easy to defend, but hard of access for the enemy; or a fortification. The flank should be hard to carry by open assault or to turn. If there are no such secure points of support, a reserve should be kept in rear of the flank to be guarded, ready to oppose any flank attack that may be made.

Q. If possible, what should be the nature of the ground in rear of the position?

A. It should be such as to offer a succession of good defensive positions, each susceptible of occupation in turn.

Q. Give a summary of the requirements of a perfect defensive position.

A. I. It should have a clear field of fire to the front and flanks.

II. The ground in its front should be such as to impede the enemy without affording him shelter from fire.

III. There should be no points in its front which could be advantageously occupied by the enemy.

Should such points exist, they should either be held as advanced posts or destroyed.

IV. It should be suitable in extent to the size of the force which occupies it.

V. Its flanks should rest securely upon defensible objects.

VI. It should have good lateral communications; such that the different parts of the front may be able to assist each other.

VII. It should furnish good cover for the troops.

VIII. It should be such as to admit of the concealment of the strength and composition of the force occupying it.

IX. It should cover the line of retreat squarely.

X. The terrain should be adapted to the action of that arm in which the defender is proportionately strongest or superior to the enemy; and it should be such as to facilitate the assumption of the offensive at an opportune moment.

Q. What in general is the best order of battle for a defensive position?

A. The concave, as it always enables a converging, and at close quarters a flanking, fire to bear on the attack.

Q. Of what three stages does the defense consist?

A. Of the preparatory stage, of the defense proper, and of the counter-attack (withdrawal, in case of defeat). In the preparatory stage, as soon as the heads of columns come within range, the batteries told off for the purpose open fire on them, but the guns in the main line are not brought up before the assailant's artillery takes up the reconnoitering position. Even then, only as many guns are brought up as may be needed to make the enemy deploy, for it is important to avoid betraying the nature and extent of the position. A part of the infantry is deployed as skirmishers in front of the batteries, but the main body is held in hand, sheltered as much as possible, until the time comes for effective employment. The cavalry and the horse artillery are on the flanks to guard against flank attacks, and to be ready to make them themselves, should opportunity offer.

The real defense, or defense proper, comes off when the hostile infantry reaches the third zone, when that of the defense must be in position. As the real attack is now developed, the infantry must be reinforced at critical points, and the artillery, ignoring the hostile guns, fires on the enemy's infantry. The cavalry on the flanks seeks an opportunity to make flank attacks, as when shattering losses or the exhaustion of ammunition deprive the hostile infantry of a large measure of its powers of resistance.

As the enemy approaches for the final charge, the entire first line is merged in the firing line, which opens rapid fire, while the second line is held in readiness to charge to meet the enemy at the moment of collision. The cavalry and the horse artillery assist the third line in the counter-attack according to principles already described. In case of defeat, the withdrawal is made as in the case of the attack.

Night Attacks.

Q. What are the advantages and disadvantages of night attacks?

A. The advantages are:

1. The fire of the enemy is encountered only at short range, and the dispositions for attack may therefore be much simplified.

2. The enemy is taken by surprise.

The disadvantages are:

1. The attacking columns are liable to lose their way in the dark.

2. The different columns are in danger of mistaking each other for the enemy, thus not only incurring loss at their own hands, but giving warning to the enemy.

3. The concentration of troops in the dark is very difficult and likely to lead to great confusion.

4. The ground cannot be so well known to the assailant as to the defender.

Q. What is an essential condition for the success of night attacks?

A. That the terrain over which they are to be made shall be accurately known; otherwise the attack is more than likely to fail. Leaders should know thoroughly what they are each to do, and there should be a watchword to enable the different columns to identify one another on meeting. Lateral communications between the attacking columns should be maintained.

Q. To what sort of forces are night attacks best suited?

A. To small forces; for the visibility and noise increase with the size of the attacking columns, and thus tend to defeat the object of the night attack.

Q. How may the concealment afforded by darkness be utilized otherwise than in night attacks?

A. In night marches; their object being to put a force in position for an attack at dawn.

Q. What arms should be used in night attacks?

A. If possible, only infantry; but artillery should

The Three Arms Combined.

be held in readiness to push forward to assist the assailing columns, as soon as the attack is developed, and there is no longer any occasion for secrecy. Cavalry cannot well be used, as the noise of the horses is largely beyond the control of the men.

Q. State the conditions under which night attacks by large forces will be advantageous.

A. 1. When the attacking army is in such spirits and rendered so audacious by previous success that it is in a condition to undertake anything.

2. When the enemy is known to be demoralized, short of ammunition, or grossly careless in the performance of his outpost duties.

3. When reinforcements are expected by the enemy, and the capture of the position is dependent upon prompt action, while an assault does not seem to be practicable by daylight.

4. For the purpose of cutting through a superior force of the enemy, in which case a surprise is necessary, and may be best effected under cover of the darkness.

PART II.
THE SERVICE OF SECURITY AND INFORMATION.

CHAPTER I.

THE ADVANCE GUARD.

Q. What would be the effect if the entire army were kept constantly on the alert?

A. Its surprise would be impossible, but it would be ruined by physical hardship. To guard against surprise without making undue demands upon the endurance of the soldiers, use is made of covering detachments, which should be strong enough to hold the enemy while the main body is preparing for action.

Q. How is the security of an army provided for on the march, and at a halt?

A. On the march the security of the army is provided for by advance guards, rear guards, and flanking detachments; at a halt a chain of outposts protects it from surprise.

Q. The information necessary for a commander is of what two kinds?

A. 1. That relating to the geography, topography, and resources of the theater of operations.

2. That which relates to the strength and composition of the enemy's forces, and their position, movements, and morale.

Q. How are these two kinds of information obtained?

A. Among military nations, the first kind of information is now generally obtained in time of peace.

The second class of information is gained in two ways:

1. From spies, deserters, prisoners, newspapers, etc.

2. By reconnaissance.

Q. What would be the effect if troops moving in one body should come suddenly upon the enemy.

A. They would certainly be thrown into confusion, and perhaps defeated, before deployment for action could be effected. Moreover, insignificant bodies of the enemy could seriously delay the march of the column by causing it to halt and deploy for action.

Q. How is a column of troops on the march, therefore, divided?

A. Into a *main body*, an *advance guard*, a *rear guard*, and such *flanking parties* as may be necessary.

Q. What are the objects of the advance guard?

A. 1. To provide for the security of the main body by giving it time for deployment when the enemy is encountered.

2. To clear the way for the main body and prevent its march from being delayed.

3. To seize and hold important points until the arrival of the main body.

4. To support the reconnoitering cavalry, and afford a rallying-point for it in case it is driven in by the enemy.

Q. How does the proportionate strength of the advance guard vary?

A. No absolute rule for the strength of the advance guard can be given, but it varies with the size of the main body, the object of the march, the topography of the country, and the nature of the enemy. In a close, rugged country, and against an enemy in-

The Advance Guard.

ferior in numbers and morale, it should be less than in an open country, against a strong, aggressive enemy, or when the intention is to bring on a decisive engagement. With a large force the proportionate strength of the advance guard is larger than in the case of a small column.

Q. As a rule, what portion of the entire force is assigned to the advance guard and to the rear guard on advance—and what on a retrograde movement?

A. As a general rule (subject, however, to a multitude of exceptions), we may assume the strength of the advance guard to be one-sixth of the whole force, and the rear guard to be half as strong as the advance guard. On a retrograde movement the relative strength of the advance and rear guards would be reversed.

Q. Into what two parts is the advance guard primarily divided, and what is the strength of each?

A. Into the *reserve* and the *vanguard*. The reserve consists of from one-third to one-half of the entire advance guard. The remainder constitutes the vanguard.

Q. Into what two parts is the vanguard divided, and what is their relative strength?

A. Into the *advance party* and the *support;* the latter being generally twice as strong as the former.

Q. How are these proportions varied?

A. In large advance guards this proportion is often different; the support, relatively to the advance party, and the reserve, relatively to the vanguard, being considerably greater. These proportions are, moreover, varied according to the most convenient subdivisions of the organizations composing the advance guard. They may be regarded as suitable in most cases.

(For a typical formation of a company of infantry as an advance guard, see Plate 7.)

Q. What may be given as a typical formation for the advance party when the advance guard consists of a company?

A. The advance party, consisting of one section, throws forward a "point" consisting of three or four men under a non-commissioned officer. On each side a flanking group of four men marches about 150 yards from the main route to the right and left rear respectively of the point. Each flanking group should be under a corporal or old soldier, and would habitually march with two men in front and one in rear of the group-leader, though the formation adopted would depend upon circumstances. The rest of the advance party follows 100 yards in rear of the point.

Q. How is the support formed, and how does it march?

A. The support (one section) follows the advance party at a distance of 200 yards, throwing out two flanking groups of four men each to its right and left front, and somewhat farther out than the flankers of the advance party. A connecting file, detached from the advance party, marches between the advance party and the support to aid in the transmission of intelligence from one to the other.

Q. How is the reserve formed, and how does it march?

A. The reserve marches about 500 yards in rear of the support, a connecting file marching between them. The reserve may throw flanking groups to the

The Advance Guard. 103

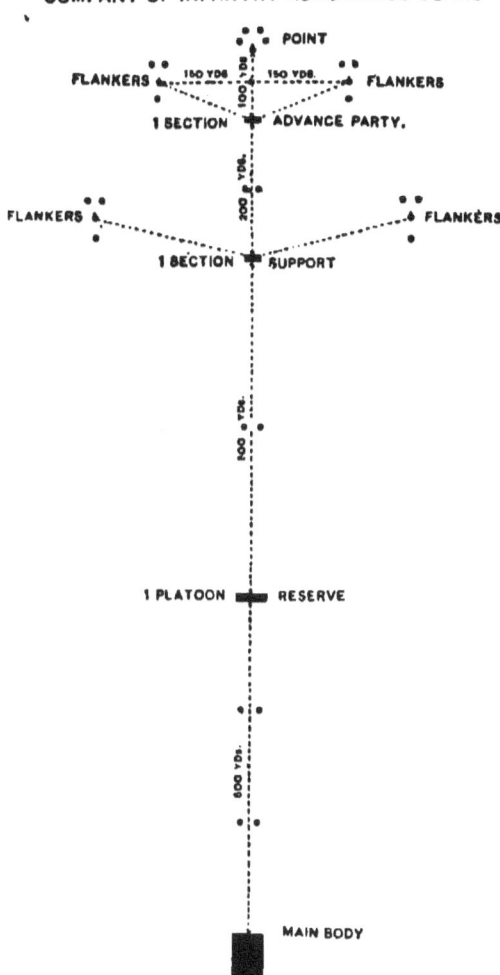

PLATE 7.

front or to the front and rear, but, the groups being slightly farther out than those of the support, as a rule, the reserve should be kept entire and well in hand.

Q. Where does the main body march?

A. The main body follows the reserve at 500 yards, one or two connecting files marching between the two bodies.

Q. Are the distances (as given above) invariable?

A. No, they are variable; but those from the support to the reserve, and from the reserve to the main body, can not prudently be made more than 600 or 800 yards, respectively, in the case of so small a force as the one considered.

Q. If the nature of the country is such as to render the use of flanking groups impracticable, what is done?

A. Both the advance party and the support move forward entire, with the exception that the advance party is always preceded by a point.

Q. When marching in an open country, how may the advance party be formed?

A. It may be deployed as skirmishers, with considerable intervals, the support following in line of squads. The reserve should ordinarily be kept in column.

Q. What might result if the distance of the advance guard from the main body were too great, and what, if it were too small?

A. If the distance were too great, the advance guard might be forced into a heavy engagement while beyond the assistance of the main body, and might even be entirely cut off by an attack upon its flank and rear. If, on the other hand, the distance were not great enough, time could not be afforded for the preparation of the main body for action.

Q. Give a rough rule which will answer in most cases for determining the distance of the advance guard from the main body.

A. A rough rule is, that the *minimum* distance should be equal to the depth of the main body; as the time required for the rear troops to deploy on the head of the column would not be greater than that taken by the advance guard in falling back.

Q. When a large force is acting with energy and aggressiveness for the purpose of bringing on a battle, what is the rule?

A. The main body must be drawn nearer to the advance guard, as the latter must be promptly supported.

Q. How do the nature of the country and state of the weather affect this distance?

A. If the country is full of defensive positions, such as to admit of a sturdy delaying action on the part of the advance guard, the distance may be decreased. In foggy weather, or at night, or during a storm of rain or snow, the distance should be decreased, as well as the front covered by the scouting groups or flanking parties. If, on the other hand, the country is open, the weather clear, and there is danger of the advance guard being driven back, the distance must be increased.

Q. What important fact must be constantly considered in regard to the vanguard and the reserve?

A. That the vanguard is the *reconnoitering* part, and the reserve essentially the *fighting* part, of the advance guard. The reserve is therefore the first body that really demands time for deployment.

Q. By whom is the vanguard commanded?

A. The vanguard should always be commanded by an officer, who should be mounted, if possible, and furnished with a detailed map of the region through which the force is marching.

Q. What is the chief duty of the commander of the vanguard.

A. To see that the proper road is taken; to cause necessary repairs to be made in roads, bridges, approaches to fords, etc.; and to see that the march of the column is not, under any circumstances, unnecessarily delayed.

Q. Where does the commander of the advance guard march?

A. He is generally with the reserve; but, on approaching the enemy, should go wherever his presence is most needed. He should always be mounted, if practicable, even in the case of a small advance guard.

Q. What qualities does the commander of the advance guard need, and why?

A. Courage, self-reliance, and good judgment. A timid officer in command of an advance guard would suffer the column to be delayed by small parties of the enemy; a rash one would plunge into combat, and might thus impose upon his superior a course of action at total variance with his plans.

Q. What should the commander of the advance guard continually consider, and what, in general, should he do?

A. He should continually consider the measures necessary for the security of the march, and for rapidly gaining reliable information of the enemy. He should carefully observe the ground, and consider the tactical use that might be made of it, and should have a clear idea as to what he intends to do in case the enemy is encountered.

Q. What is done when the advance guard halts?

A. All approaches should be reconnoitered and guarded, and an officer should be sent to get an extended view from the highest available point. During a short halt, each part of the advance guard remains in the place where it is halted. If a prolonged halt is contemplated, it occupies ground that will furnish a good defensive position.

Q. How is information conveyed from one part of the advance guard to another?

A. By some code of signals. Shouting and unnecessary firing should be carefully avoided. The point and flankers fire only when they are certain that they have been seen by the enemy and that he is not retiring.

Q. How does a cavalry advance guard compare with one composed of infantry?

A. It is similar in its formation, except that the distances and intervals are greater.

Q. Why are the distances and intervals greater in the case of a cavalry advance guard than in one composed of infantry?

A. Cavalry possessing much greater mobility than infantry, the different covering troops can be safely separated from each other by greater distances in the former than in the latter arm. Moreover, the resisting power of cavalry is less than that of infantry, and when a cavalry advance guard is driven in by the enemy, the ground is passed over more rapidly in retreat than in the case of a corresponding infantry force. Hence, in order to give each successive body in rear time to prepare for action, the distances must necessarily be greater for cavalry.

Q. Why should an advance guard be composed of all arms?

A. Because reconnoitering duty can be performed more efficiently and more easily by cavalry than by infantry; because infantry has more resisting power than the cavalry; and because artillery is of great value in preparing the way for the advance guard and in compelling the enemy to deploy at a distance.

Q. How would the different arms be distributed in the advance guard?

A. The cavalry would constitute the vanguard, and the infantry the reserve. The artillery would habitually be with the reserve, though in some cases a few guns might march with the support.

Q. How are engineers used with the advance guard?

A. A few engineers should march with the support, to repair bridges, remove obstacles, etc.

Q. Upon what does the proportion of each arm with the advance guard depend, and when is each preferable?

A. It depends upon the nature of the country, the object of the march, and the strength, composition, and proximity of the enemy. In close or mountainous country, the proportion of infantry should be increased. In an open country the cavalry should be strengthened. If the enemy is strong and near, and a battle seems imminent, the advance guard should be very strong in infantry and guns. If, however, it is desired merely to develop the enemy without seriously engaging, the advance guard should consist of cavalry and light artillery (horse artillery, if possible), as these troops can be more readily withdrawn than infantry. In the pursuit of a beaten foe, or whenever the object is to follow and keep touch with the enemy, the proportion of cavalry should be as great as possible.

Q. What should be done by the advance guard when the enemy is encountered?

A. As soon as the enemy is seen, the advance guard must endeavor to ascertain promptly whether it has to deal with an outpost of a stationary force, an advance guard of a marching body, or a flanking detachment of a column. It should lose no time in discovering where the enemy's main position is, or how far away is the marching column. The relative numbers and position and the orders under which the advance guard is acting will decide the question of attacking or taking up a defensive position. The offensive is generally the best if an attack seems at all likely to succeed. If it be decided to attack, the reserve will reinforce the support if the defensive has been decided upon, or if the enemy is in such force that the advance guard can not hold its own against him, it will be necessary to fall back slowly and stubbornly to a defensive position or upon the main body.

CHAPTER II.

Outposts in General.

Q. What are outposts, and with what duties are they charged?

A. Outposts are detachments thrown out from a force when halted, for the purpose of protecting it from surprise. Like advance guards on the march, outposts are charged with the duties of observation and resistance. They prevent the reconnaissance of the position by the enemy's scouts and patrols, give warning of the approach of hostile bodies, and offer sufficient resistance to the enemy's attacks to enable the main body to prepare for action.

Q. What effect has a system of outposts on the health and efficiency of an army?

A. Unbroken rest at night being necessary for the preservation of the health and efficiency of troops undergoing the hardships and fatigues of a campaign, it is of the utmost importance that the repose of the army in camp or bivouac should not be disturbed by needless alarms. The army must feel that the vigilance of its outposts enables it to sleep in security.

Q. How may the duties of an outpost be classified.

A. The duties of the outposts may be classified as follows:
Observation:
        1. To observe constantly all approaches by which the enemy might advance.
        2. To watch, and immediately report, the movements of the enemy.

Outposts in General.

Resistance:

    1. To prevent reconnaissance by the enemy.

    2. *Above all*, to check the advance of the enemy long enough to enable the main body to prepare for action.

Q. Into what parts is an outpost divided?

A. Into four parts, namely: 1. Sentinels or vedettes; 2. Pickets; 3. Supports; 4. Reserve.

Q. Who occupy the line of observation, and who the line of resistance?

A. The sentinels or vedettes* occupy the *line of observation*. They are sent out from the pickets, and supported by them. The supports usually occupy the *line of resistance*, and are supported by the reserve.

Q. What are the normal distances between the subdivisions of an outpost of infantry, of cavalry?

A. In an infantry outpost the pickets are from 100 to 400 yards in rear of the sentinels; the supports, from 400 to 800 yards in rear of the pickets; and the reserve, from 400 to 800 yards in rear of the supports. In a cavalry outpost the distance from the vedettes to the picket is about 600 yards, and the other distances vary between the limits of 1200 and 2000 yards. These distances can not be definitely fixed, as they depend upon many circumstances of ground, weather, and the nature and proximity of the enemy.

Q. To what may the general plan of an outpost be likened?

A. To an open fan, the sentinels being along the outer edge; or, better yet, to a hand with the fingers extended and widely opened. A line along the tips of

---

*A vedette is a mounted sentinel.

the fingers would represent the chain of sentinels; the first joints, the line of pickets; the second joints, the line of supports; and the knuckles, the line of the reserve; while the wrist would represent the position of the main body. (See Plate 8.)

Q. What portion of the strength of the outpost is generally assigned to the reserve, to the supports, and to the pickets?

A. The reserve generally consists of not less than one-third nor more than one-half of the entire outpost. The strength of the supports and pickets would consequently vary from two-thirds to one-half of the outpost.

Q. On what does the strength of a picket depend, and what principle regulates the strength of each support?

A. The strength of each picket depends upon the number of sentinels and patrols that it has to furnish, and the size of each support is regulated by the principle that it should be equal to the aggregate strength of all the pickets supported by it. As a general rule, one-third of the outposts would be assigned to the reserve, one-third to the supports, and one-third to the pickets and sentries.

Q. What two systems of outposts are there, and what are their general characteristics?

A. Outposts are of two kinds: the *cordon* system, in which the entire front is covered with a chain of sentinels; and the *patrol* system, in which only the roads and other avenues of approach are guarded by sentinels, closely backed up by pickets, while the intervening country is constantly patrolled. The best results are generally obtained by a combination of the two systems.

Outposts in General. 113

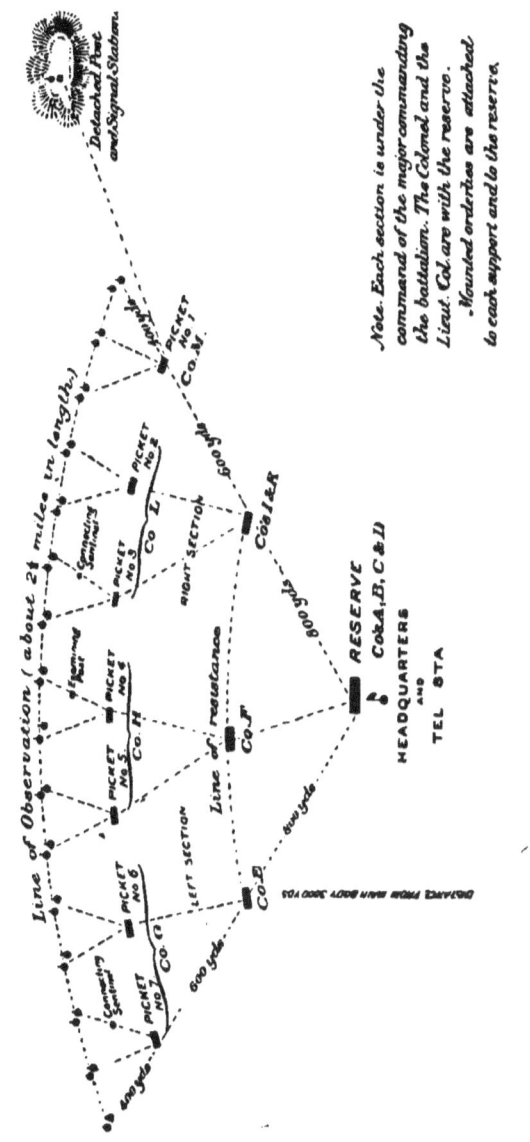

PLATE 8.

Q. State the requirements of a good outpost position.

A. The outpost must cover the front of the army and overlap its flanks, unless the latter are secured by impassable obstacles. A prominent natural feature should be selected to mark the general line, such as a ridge, a river, or the farther edge of a wood. The most favorable position is one which furnishes a good view and field of fire to the front, while affording concealment from the enemy and shelter from his fire.

Q. State what furnishes one of the best, and what one of the worst, outpost positions.

A. One of the best positions is a wood held at the edge toward the enemy, and one of the worst is a wood held at the nearer edge.

Q. What should generally be the shape of the outpost line?

A. It should be convex towards the enemy, or straight with its extremities thrown back. Unless the nature of the ground compels, it should never be concave, even when that is the shape of the position which it covers. It does not necessarily conform strictly to the line of the position in any case.

Q. On what does the strength of the outpost depend?

A. Upon various considerations, such as the nature of the country and the strength, proximity, and character of the enemy. In a country well adapted to defense, smaller numbers suffice than in an open country. When the enemy is near and aggressive, the outposts must be strong and vigilant. The strength of the outpost will also depend upon the plan of action determined upon in case of attack. If the line chosen for the deployment of the main body coincides with the line of resistance of the outpost, the latter force must be strong enough to hold the chosen position to the utmost. If it is decided to fall back upon the main body, the outpost not only may be, but should be, weaker than in the former case, as a strong force would be more likely to become compromised in a serious engagement than a weaker one.

Q. As a rule, what is the maximum strength of an outpost in proportion to the entire command?

A. As a rule, the maximum strength of an outpost is one-sixth of the entire force. This proportion should not be exceeded, except in case of absolute necessity, and it should be less whenever a reduction is consistent with prudence.

Q. When the army is marching, from day to day, what constitutes the outpost at each halt?

A. When an army is on the march from day to day, the advance guard constitutes the outpost at each halt; but if its duties during the day's march have been arduous, it must be relieved, as soon as practicable, by fresh troops.

Q. If outposts are required on the flanks and rear, of what are they composed?

A. They are composed of the flank and rear guards, when such guards exist in sufficient strength; otherwise such outposts are taken from the main body, which will also furnish them when the duties of the flank and rear guards during the day have been especially trying.

(For a typical disposition of a regiment of infantry forming the outpost of a division, see Plate 8.)

Q. In the disposition of an outpost, what attention is paid to the different tactical units?

A. They should, as far as practicable, be kept intact. Thus, supposing the outposts of a division to consist of a regiment of infantry, the reserve might be composed of the first battalion; the support, of two companies of the second battalion and two of the third, each supporting the remaining companies of its own battalion, which would constitute the pickets and sentinels. (See Plate 8.)

(For a typical disposition of a squadron of cavalry forming the outpost of a cavalry brigade, see Plate 9.)

Q. How are the outposts for divisions and brigades generally furnished?

A. Each division will generally furnish the outposts for its own front. In a large force especially this principle may be advantageously applied to brigades. In this case the outpost of the division might consist of a battalion (four companies) from each of the three brigades.

Q. What provisions for the command of the outpost are made in this case?

A. The outpost of each brigade would be under the command of the officer commanding the battalion composing it, and would constitute a section of the general outpost. An officer should be detailed to command the entire outpost.

Q. When is infantry preferable to cavalry for outpost duty, and the reserve, and how may the two arms be advantageously combined.

A. In an open country, in daytime, the duty can be best performed by cavalry. In a close country, at night, and when the enemy is near, infantry is preferable. The best performance of outpost duty requires a combination of the two arms. Cavalry is of

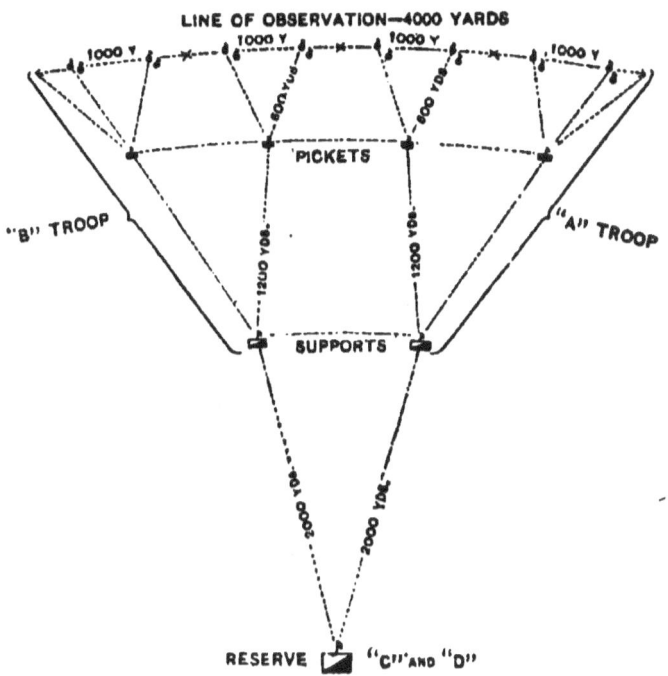

PLATE 9.

the greatest value when pushed well to the front as a screen, but it may often be advantageously combined with infantry in the outpost proper. It may thus occupy lookout stations too distant to be held by infantry, or patrol to a distance beyond the outpost that would be impracticable for the latter arm. As a rule, when it is impracticable to use the cavalry as an advanced screen, its use with the outposts should be limited to patrolling and to furnishing orderlies, when necessary, to the pickets, supports, and reserve.

Q. How should artillery be used with an outpost?

A. Artillery is of great value to an outpost when it can be so posted as to command an important road or defile and be at the same time beyond the effective range of the enemy's rifle fire. When not posted to command bridges or roads, it should be with the reserve, preferably near a road.

Q. What considerations determine the distance of the outpost from the main body?

A. The outpost must be far enough from the main body to give the latter time to form for action before the outlying troops are driven in. On the other hand, it must not be so far distant as to be in danger of being cut off by the enemy. The distance will also depend upon the strength that can be spared for the outpost line, the length of the line increasing almost in direct proportion with the distance.

Q. What is the usual distance, and what is the maximum distance?

A. The supports (occupying the line of resistance) should be at a distance of about 3000 yards from the main body. This fixes the line of supports, at proper distances from which the other parts of the outpost are established. The maximum distance from an infantry outpost to the body which it covers is about 3 miles, supposing the outpost to be of considerable strength and strongly posted.

Q. How is the outpost divided, and where are the several headquarters?

A. The officer detailed to command the outpost makes his headquarters with the reserve, and establishes there his field telegraph or signal station. If the front of the outpost is considerable, it is divided into sections of about a mile or a mile and a half for infantry and three miles for cavalry, and an officer assigned to the command of each section. Each section commander makes his headquarters with one of his supports, and is under the orders of the commander of the outpost.

Q. What instructions does the outpost commander receive from the commander of the forces, and what does he (the outpost commander) then do?

A. The outpost commander receives from the commander of the forces instructions as to the general front to be occupied by the outposts, their object, and the amount of resistance they are expected to make. He is also informed about the avenues of approach from the direction of the opposing force, and is made acquainted with everything known in regard to the position and probable intentions of the enemy. He then determines the strength of the reserve, supports, and pickets; decides upon the distance of the line of resistance from the main body, and selects a line of observation farther in advance. The station of the reserve is next fixed, the positions of the supports pointed out, places for the pickets approximately designated, and the general line of the sentinels roughly indicated.

Q. What instructions does the outpost commander give to his subordinates?

A. He instructs them as to:

1. The general front of the outpost line.
2. The ground to be occupied by each.
3. The positions of neighboring supports and pickets.
4. The night positions of the pickets and supports.
5. What is known of the enemy and his probable movements.
6. The approaches by which the enemy might advance.
7. The direction and method of patrolling.
8. What is to be done in case of attack.
9. How flags of truce and deserters are to be received.
10. The kind of reports required.
11. Where he himself is to be found.
12. The countersign and parole.

Q. When the outpost has been posted, what does its commander do?

A. When the outpost has been posted, its commander makes his inspection; orders such changes in the positions of supports, pickets, or sentinels as may seem advisable; sees that the roads and paths leading from the enemy are properly guarded; gives directions for the fortification of such parts of the position as need strengthening; and is especially careful that the flanks are secured by resting them on impassable obstacles, or by refusing them and protecting them by detachments.

CHAPTER III.

Sentinels and Pickets.—Supports, Reserve.— The Outpost at Night.

Q. How are sentinels generally posted, and how may the group system be used?

A. Sentinels must be so posted as to have a good view to the front and flanks, and be concealed as much as possible. They do not walk their posts, but remain stationary, being generally posted double, so that one man may go to examine any suspicious point while the other remains on post. They may also be posted in groups. In the former case the reliefs not on post remain with the picket; in the latter case the group accompanies the sentinel to his post and remains in concealment a short distance behind him. When the group system is used, a single sentinel for each will suffice by day, but double sentinels should be used at night. As the group furnishes the reliefs, it should consist of three or six men, and every two or three groups should be under the charge of a non-commissioned officer.

Q. What are the most important requirements of a good post for a sentinel?

A. There should be easy communication with neighboring sentinels and with the picket, and a clear view of all approaches.

Q. How far apart may sentinels and vedettes be? —minimum and maximum distances?

A. Sentinels are generally not less than 100 nor more than 400 yards apart—the lesser limit being usually the minimum for single sentinels, and the greater limit the maximum for double ones. Vedettes may be as far as 600 yards apart. But no definite rule can be laid down in this matter, except that the number of posts should be sufficient to insure a vigilant watch on all points at which the enemy might approach.

Q. How are the sentinel posts numbered?

A. The posts furnished by each picket are numbered from right to left.

Q. What are the general duties of a sentinel?

A. Sentinels should watch and listen without betraying their own presence; but observation is the first consideration, and concealment is of secondary importance. They must not smoke, and such conversation as may be necessary between them must be conducted in a whisper. The sentinel must not have about him any glittering accouterments; and, except in foggy weather or on a dark night, must keep his bayonet in its scabbard.

Q. What should each sentinel clearly understand?

A. 1. The countersign.

2. The number of his own post.

3. The number and position of his own picket and the name of its commander.

4. The position of the neighboring sentinels and the examining post, where there is one.

5. The direction of the enemy and the probable line of his advance.

6. The points to which all roads, paths, and railroads in sight lead.

7. The names of all villages and rivers in view.

Sentinels and Pickets. 123

8. The signals by which he should communicate with the pickets or detached posts.

The principal thing is that he should know where to look for the enemy, and what to do if he sees him.

Q. What persons are allowed to cross the line of sentinels, and what is done with the others?

A. Only persons in the performance of duty with the outpost, or having authority over it, are allowed to cross the line of sentinels. All other people, with the exception of deserters and bearers of flags of truce, are halted, not more than one being advanced at a time, and then conducted, by one of the sentinels, back to the picket, or detained until the arrival of the visiting patrol. If they refuse to halt, or attempt to escape, they must be shot down. If there is a special examining post, people are conducted to it instead of to the picket.

Q. How are deserters from the enemy received at the outpost?

A. They are halted at some distance from the post, and required to lay down their arms. The commander of the picket is at once notified, and he sends out a patrol to bring them in.

Q. When a flag of truce approaches, how is the bearer received by the sentinel?

A. The bearer and his escort (if he have one) are halted in front of the line of sentinels and ordered to face in the direction from which they came. Word is then at once sent back to the commander of the picket. While the bearer and his escort are halted, the sentinel must not converse with them nor allow them to reconnoiter.

Q. Everything observed by the sentinel is how communicated?

A. It should be communicated at once to the picket, especial care being taken to report promptly all indications of the enemy's approach. If the sentinel is satisfied that the enemy is advancing to attack, he gives the alarm by firing.

Q. What are the general rules in regard to sentinels firing?

A. When immediate alarm is not necessary, firing should be avoided; it disturbs the repose of the troops, and if groundless alarms are frequently given, the troops grow careless and fail to heed the warning when real danger comes. The sentinel, by firing, often needlessly alarms his own outpost, and gives a certain amount of information to the enemy by betraying his own position; while by remaining hidden and watching carefully he might be able to give a valuable report of the disposition of the opposing outpost.

Q. How are sentinels posted, and how often should they be relieved?

A. It is advisable to keep the same men on the same posts, instead of changing them to new ones each time they are posted. For very important posts the most intelligent men should be selected, and on double posts the well-instructed and intelligent man is placed with one who is less so. The sentinels should be relieved every two hours during the day and every hour during the night. In very inclement weather they should be relieved every hour during the day.

Q. How are vedettes posted?

A. Vedettes, like sentinels, are posted in pairs, and for similar reasons. One is habitually 6 or 8 yards to the right or left rear of the other; a greater distance would make the horses uneasy, and thus distract the attention of the riders, while a less distance would encourage conversation between the vedettes.

Q. How may vedettes sometimes perform their duty dismounted?

A. When cavalry is operating in a close or wooded country, the vedettes may dismount, one holding the horses while the other keeps watch. The horses may sometimes be held behind the brow of a hill, while a vedette, lying down, peers over the crest.

Q. What is a connecting sentinel?

A. When the sentinel post is not in plain view of the picket, a connecting sentinel is posted at a point where he can see the post and be seen by the picket. It is his duty to transmit signals from one to the other. Connecting sentinels are always single. A connecting vedette is generally mounted by day, and always at night. If dismounted, his horse is with the picket.

Q. What is a picket sentinel?

A. A single sentinel posted at the picket to keep a lookout on the sentinels or connecting sentinels, and report all signals made by them or any unusual occurrence. In a cavalry picket this sentinel is dismounted.

Q. What are detached posts?

A. They are small parties detached from a picket to protect exposed points or support isolated sentinels. They consist generally of from three to twelve men, and are under an officer or non-commissioned officer, according to their strength and the importance of their position. They are, in fact, small pickets, and must act in concert with the pickets from which they are taken.

Q. What points may be advantageously held by detached posts?

A. A bridge on a flank might be held by a detached post. An isolated hill, affording a good outlook, too far to the front to be included in the general line, but near enough to be occupied without extreme risk, should be held by such a post, communicating with the outpost by signal.

Q. How often are detached posts relieved, and what is required of the men composing them?

A. *If practicable*, detached posts should be relieved every six hours. They are not allowed to light fires, and the men are required to keep on their equipments and have their arms constantly at hand. In a detached post composed of cavalry the horses are kept constantly saddled and bridled and held by horse-holders, three-fourths of the men being ready to fight on foot. The sentinels or dismounted vedettes are posted close in front of the party. Vedettes may be pushed farther forward.

Q. What is the usual strength of a picket, both infantry and cavalry?

A. An infantry picket generally consists of from 25 to 50 men, and a cavalry picket usually varies between 20 and 30.

Q. How many double sentinels or vedettes does a picket usually furnish?

A. From two to four double sentinels or vedettes, there being three reliefs for each post.

Q. What regulates the strength of a picket, and what portion of the picket is used in patrolling?

A. If detached posts are to be sent out from the picket, corresponding additional strength must be given it, and an allowance must be made for patrolling. The requirements for patrolling vary so much that the proportion of the picket to be used for that purpose can not be fixed. Generally, about a third of the picket, should be used in patrolling. In a close country, the patrols, rather than the sentinels, should be increased; and at night the patrols are the principal reliance for observation. There should be enough men for three patrols, so as to admit of one patrol being out, one *ready* to go out, and one resting. This is especially the case with a cavalry picket. The strength of the picket will thus vary; but its *minimum* strength must allow six men for every double-sentinel post, three for each connecting sentinel, three for the picket sentinel, and at least three non-commissioned officers. These are the barest requirements, without considering patrols. The picket commander should always, if possible, be a commissioned officer.

Q. What are the maximum and minimum fronts of an infantry picket?

A. The minimum front covered by the sentinels of a single picket may be placed at 400 yards. The maximum front, even when the picket furnishes four double sentinels, may be placed at 800 yards.

Q. What are the maximum and minimum fronts of a cavalry picket?

A. The front covered by the vedettes of a cavalry picket varies from 1000 to 2000 yards.

Q. Pickets are generally about how far apart?

A. Infantry pickets are generally from 600 to 800 yards apart, and cavalry pickets from 1000 to 1500 yards. All these distances vary with different circumstances of ground and weather; the distances given above have been found by experience to answer in many cases, but they must often be materially changed.

Q. What line is the first consideration in selecting the ground for the outpost?

A. The line of resistance should be made the first consideration in selecting the ground for the outpost; then the line of observation should be fixed, the position of the sentinels regulating that of the pickets, and not the reverse.

Q. What are the six requirements of a perfect picket post?

A. 1. It should be near enough to the sentinels to give them prompt support, but not so close as to be involved in their disaster if they should be surprised and suddenly driven in;

2. It should be posted on, and command, some route leading from the enemy; the largest pickets on the most important routes;

3. It should be in good defensive position, should have a good field of fire to the front, and should be so far concealed that the enemy could not discover it without attacking;

4. It should, as far as consistent with the foregoing requirements, be in rear of the center of its line of sentinels;

5. It should have free approaches to its sentinels, neighboring pickets, supports, and reserves, and should have a good line of retreat;

6. It should be close enough to the neighboring pickets for mutual support, and a mutual flanking fire should be provided for.

A position fulfilling all these requirements can scarcely be hoped for; the best position will be the one which fulfills the greatest part of them.

Q. When an impassable obstacle lies along a portion of the front of the outpost, what may be done?

A. When an impassable obstacle, such as a swamp, lake, or stream, lies along a portion of the front of the outposts, the strength at that part of the line may be limited to the requirements of observation, the sentinels being few, and the chief reliance being placed upon patrolling.

Q. What are the general rules concerning fires with the pickets?

A. Fires should not be lighted by a picket unless they can be well concealed from the enemy.

Q. What is required of the men composing the picket, both infantry and cavalry?

A. The men composing the picket stack arms and may remove their equipments, with the exception of the cartridge-belt. They must not leave the immediate vicinity of the picket, and must be ready to fall in at a moment's notice. Part of the men must be constantly under arms at night, and separated from the rest, who keep their arms close at hand while sleeping. If danger seems imminent, the entire picket must be awake and under arms. In a cavalry picket, or in the case of mounted orderlies attached to an infantry picket, the horses should be kept constantly saddled, and the bridles should be taken off only for feeding and watering. Not more than one-third, or at most one-half, of the horses should be fed at a time.

Q. What do the supports constitute?

A. The supports constitute a force upon which the pickets fall back if driven in by the enemy, or with which (in exceptional cases) the pickets may be reinforced.

Q. What regulates the position of the supports, and what should be its general requirements?

A. The ground regulates their position, as they should occupy the line of resistance. The position selected should afford a good general line of defense, ground uniformly moderately good being preferable to that which is very strong in some parts and weak in others. The supports should not be too far away from the pickets to render timely aid, nor so close as to be involved in their defeat if suddenly driven in. They should be located as centrally as practicable in reference to the pickets in their front, and should preferably be upon, or near, the main routes by which the enemy might advance. Sometimes the best line of resistance lies close to the line of observation, or even coincides with it. In such cases the supports may be close to the pickets or merged with them. One support is generally sufficient for two or three pickets.

Q. What is required of the men composing the support?

A. The support should have one or more sentinels or vedettes posted the same as a picket, but may relax to some extent the watchfulness exacted from the pickets. The men stack arms and are allowed to remove their accouterments (excepting always the cartridge-belt), but they are not permitted to wander away from the post of the support, and must be ready at all times to fall in. They are usually allowed to light fires, and may be required to do the cooking for the pickets as well as themselves. The horses with the support are kept in the same degree of readiness as those with the pickets. No shouting or unnecessary noise of any kind should be permitted in any part of the outpost.

Q. What are Cossack posts?

A. They are small posts sent out directly from the supports. Each of these posts consists of four men; namely, three reliefs of a single sentinel, and a non-commissioned officer or old soldier for the command of the post.

Q. How many Cossack posts are furnished by each support, and how are they placed?

A. Each support furnishes from four to twelve Cossack posts, which are placed from 300 to 400 yards in advance of it, and from 100 to 300 yards apart; the smaller limit of distance in the case of very close and rugged ground, and the latter in the case of very open ground. The sentinel is stationed from 10 to 30 yards in advance of the post, the other members of which remain concealed and keep him constantly in view. (See Plate 10.)

Q. How often are the sentinels and posts relieved, and how is the patrolling done

A. The sentinels are relieved every hour and the post every three hours. One or two men may be sent from the post from time to time, to patrol to the post on either side; but, as a rule, all the patrolling is done from the support.

Q. Should either the picket system or Cossack posts be exclusively employed?

A. Not as a rule. A combination of the two is usually preferable. If a wood or a broken piece of ground exists in the line, Cossack posts would generally be more suitable; but on the open ground the picket system would usually be preferable.

132 Elements of Military Science.

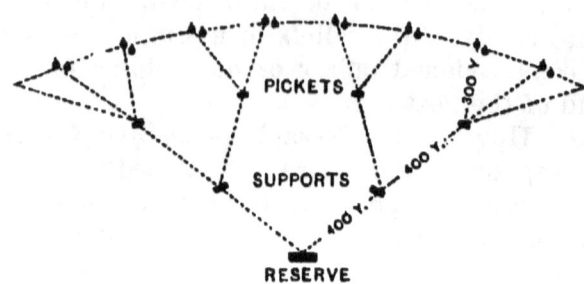

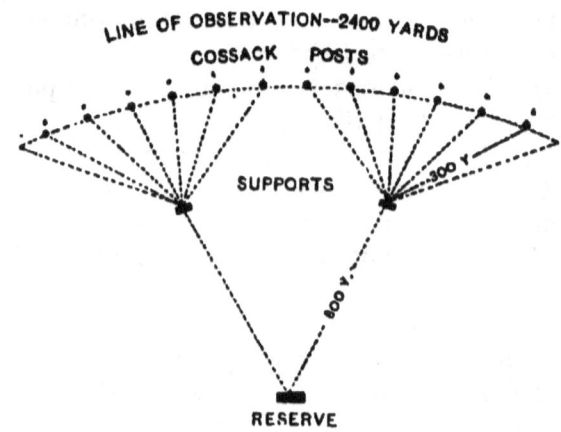

PLATE 10.

Sentinels and Pickets. 133

Q. What does the reserve constitute, and of what does it generally consist?

A. It constitutes the general support and pivot of resistance of the whole outpost, and usually consists of all three arms.

Q. What considerations influence the selection of its position?

A. It should be concealed from the enemy, and should be posted as centrally as practicable, so as to enable it to move quickly to any endangered point. It may sometimes be divided into two parts, to facilitate supporting the more advanced bodies; and it should be upon the prinicpal line or lines of retreat to the main body.

Q. What rules obtain in regard to the men and horses of the reserve?

A. The same as in the case of the supports. The reserve is allowed to light fires; and in the exceptional cases where fires are prohibited to the more advanced parties, it must do the cooking for them.

Q. When may the reserve be dispensed with?

A. In the case of a small force which can prepare quickly for action, or when the main body bivouacs in order of battle, the reserve may sometimes be dispensed with.

Q. What is the objection to retaining the cordon system at night?

A. It would be necessary either to increase the number of sentinels greatly, thus adding to the burden of outpost duty, or else to draw in the outpost line closer to the main body, thus contracting the front.

Q. What system is generally adopted, in its essential features, at night; and on what is it based?

A. The outpost system of Marshal Bugeaud is generally adopted in its essential features for night. This is based on the idea that in making a night attack, in any but an exceptionally open country, the enemy's movements must necessarily be confined to roads and clearly defined paths.

Q. Give the important details of the outpost system at night.

A. If double sentinels are placed on the roads and paths, and closely backed up by their reliefs, the advanced posts thus formed will give timely warning of the enemy's approach in force. But the intervening ground must not be neglected, or hostile patrols might push through and reconnoiter the position. The ground between the sentinels is, therefore, thoroughly patrolled, the number of men available for this purpose being increased by the diminution of the number of sentinel posts. Nothing more than careful observation and warning should be expected of the advanced posts, the duty of resistance falling first upon the pickets, which should be nearer the sentinels at night than during the day, and should be in strong defensive positions on the roads, in rear of the advanced posts furnished by them.

Q. In cavalry outposts, where are the pickets posted at night, and what precautions are taken?

A. In cavalry outposts, the pickets are placed on the roads, double vedettes being pushed out in front. The picket must be on the alert and prepared to fight on foot. Its position may be strengthened by barricading the road; but care must be taken to leave a passage by which the vedettes may retire, and the barcle to the advance of the troops in rear.

ricade must not be so constructed as to prove an obsta-

Q. When are the changes in the position of the outpost arranged and made?

A. All changes in the position of the outpost must be arranged during daylight, and made at late dusk. Even if the cordon system is retained and the line is not drawn in, the positions of the sentinels and pickets should be changed, in order to prevent their possible capture by the enemy, who may have noted their positions during the day.

Q. What change is made in the positions of the sentinels for night?

A. The sentinels, who are habitually posted on high ground during the day, should be moved to lower ground at night, so as to bring an approaching enemy in view on the sky line.

CHAPTER IV.

OUTPOST PATROLS.—HOW OUTPOSTS ARE POSTED AND RELIEVED.

Q. Of what two kinds are the outpost patrols?

A. Visiting patrols and reconnoitering patrols.

Q. What are the composition and duties of a visiting patrol?

A. Visiting patrols usually consist of a non-commissioned officer and two or three men. They are sent out from the picket, and keep up communication between it and its sentinels and detached posts, the neighboring pickets, and the support. They examine any suspicious points which the sentinel can not inspect without going too far away from his post, take charge of persons detained by the sentinels, and relieve any sentinel who may be sick or wounded.

Q. When are visiting patrols mainly used, and what extent of front do they cover?

A. Visiting patrols are mainly used at night. When the sentinels can be seen from the picket, the patrol would not ordinarily make the rounds, during the day, oftener than once each relief. At night, the patrol should not cover a front of more than 500 yards in its operations. When the picket is weak, the reliefs must be used as visiting patrols.

Q. What is the object of reconnoitering patrols?

A. The sentinels guard against surprise, but the information they can gain in regard to the enemy is generally very slight. This information must be sought by reconnoitering patrols sent out towards the enemy, to watch his movements, and, if possible, examine his position.

Q. What is the size of reconnoitering patrols, and how far do they go beyond the line of sentinels?

A. Reconnoitering patrols are either *small* or *strong*. A small patrol varies in size from three men to a squad. If composed of infantry, it should not, as a rule, advance more than half a mile beyond the line of sentinels at night; in daytime it may often prudently advance farther. Cavalry is generally used for this duty by day, and may push out five or ten miles, or even farther, according to the discretion of the patrol commander.

Q. What patrols should be used at night, and what must be constantly varied in regard to them?

A. It is a good rule to use at night the patrols that have scouted the same region by day. The time, direction, and manner of sending out patrols must be constantly varied, in order that the enemy may not be prepared to cut them off. A small patrol must constantly bear in mind that its business is not to fight, but to observe. It should accordingly be careful to avoid engagements, unless ordered to take prisoners.

Q. When is the duty of a reconnoitering patrol best performed?

A. When it comes back with valuable information without having been seen by the enemy.

Q. What are patrolling posts?

A. They are small patrols, of four men each, which are sometimes used at night instead of the advanced posts in front of the pickets.

Q. How does the patrolling post perform its duties?

A. It must not leave the road or path assigned to it; but it may either keep moving or remain stationary at the distance to which it is ordered to patrol. In the latter case a sentinel or vedette is posted and the rest of the patrol remains near at hand and well concealed.

Q. From what part of the outpost are strong patrols taken, and how do they vary in size?

A. They are generally taken from the support or reserve. They vary in size from nine men to a company or troop; and if composed of less than two squads, may be taken from a picket.

Q. How far from the line of sentinels may a strong patrol advance, and how may it sometimes be used

A. As a rule, the movements of a strong patrol are not so cautious as those of a small one. Its object is to gain information that can not be acquired by sentinels or small patrols. It rarely goes more than a mile and a half from the line of sentinels, and if composed of infantry, it should have one or two mounted men (or cyclists, in suitable country) with it to insure the rapid transmission of intelligence back to the outpost. If the patrols return without reporting anything, vigilance must not be relaxed; for it is possible for patrols to take a wrong direction, or to pass close to the enemy without discovering him.

Q. With what should the men detailed for outpost duty be supplied?

A. They should have a proper supply of ammunition, and (when practicable) one day's cooked rations. Their canteens should be filled with coffee.

Q. How is the posting of the outpost conducted?

A. The troops detailed having been inspected,

and the subordinate officers having taken down in writing the instructions of the outpost commander (if time admits), the force moves out, with an advance guard, to take up the designated positions. The reserve and supports may each march independently from the camp directly to its position; or they may march together and be detached from the column at suitable points. Each body moves to its position covered by a point and flanking groups, and the pickets especially move with extreme vigilance. When the picket is halted, slightly in rear of the selected line of observation, two or more squads are deployed as skirmishers, with sufficient intervals to enable their front to cover approximately the front of the sentinels of the picket, and are pushed forward cautiously to reconnoiter, being followed by the first relief of sentinels. The picket commander halts on the line of observation, and the skirmishers move on to reconnoiter in its front, not going farther than 100 yards if the country is close or wooded. When the relief comes up, the picket commander posts the sentinels quickly, the posts afterwards being changed as maybe required. Any tree, building, haystack, or other object affording a good view should be occupied at once as a lookout by two men, one of whom should, if practicable, be provided with a field-glass. As soon as the sentinels have been tentatively posted, the skirmishers are recalled and sent back to the picket; after which the picket commander touches upon the nearest sentinel of the picket on his right (or left), and passes along his own line of observation to the nearest sentinel of the picket on his left (or right). He assures himself that his sentinels are in positions best suited for observation and concealment, sees that the number of posts does not exceed the requirements of efficient observation, and then returns to his picket. He then posts such connecting and picket sentinels and detached posts as may be necessary, details a portion of the picket for patrol duty, orders the picket to stack arms and fall out, and sends to the commander of the outpost or section a report of his position and dispositions, accompanied, if practicable, with a hasty sketch or map of the same.

Q. After the picket is posted, what does its commander do?

A. After the picket commander has sent in his first report, he visits his detached posts, and makes such inspection of the ground as may be necessary to familiarize him with the roads, paths, and other topographical features of his position, but should not go beyond reach of his picket. If he has not a map of the position, he should make or have made as good a one as he can for reference, report, and giving instructions to subordinates. If streams or other obstacles exist in front of his position, he ascertains at what points they are passable; and he must satisfy himself that the picket occupies a post fulfilling, as far as possible, the requirements already set forth. He takes such measures in regard to strengthening his position as may be required by circumstances and be in consonance with orders received by him. He must be especially careful to see that the picket post at night is prepared for a stubborn defense; and he must, at all times, consider what he would do in case of attack.

Q. When, at the close of the day's march, the advance guard forms the outpost, what portions of it constitute the various parts of the outpost?

A. The advance party then furnishes the pickets and sentinels (being reinforced, if necessary, from the support until the two bodies are equal in strength); the support furnishes the supports; and the reserve constitutes the reserve of the outpost. When the place for camp or bivouac is selected, the advance guard marches to its post as an outpost in the same general manner as though detailed from camp.

Q. How is the defense of an outpost conducted?

A. The outpost should, as a rule, avoid unnecessary movements tending to bring on an engagement; but if attacked, it should resist stubbornly, in order to give the main body time to prepare for action. The chief resistance is generally made on the line of supports, though in some cases it may be best for the supports to advance to the line of pickets. In the former case, the picket usually deploys as skirmishers, and advances to reinforce the line of sentinels; the whole line then falling back slowly upon the supports, taking advantage of every defensive feature of the ground, and fighting resolutely. In order that the fire of the support may not be masked, the pickets will direct their retreat upon its flanks, instead of falling directly back upon it. The skirmishers then form on a line with the skirmishers of the support. In the latter case, the pickets should be intrenched. The sentinels fall back upon them, moving towards their flanks to unmask their fire; and the supports are brought up and deployed in the intervals between the pickets. In either case, the reserve is brought up to reinforce the troops in front, as soon as the nature and direction of the attack become apparent.

Q. When should the pickets be under arms, and why?

A. They should be under arms an hour before daybreak, as an attack is most likely to occur at dawn.

Q. When is the outpost relieved?

A. The outpost is relieved at daybreak, in order that there may be double strength on the outpost line at the time when an attack is most to be feared.

Q. Describe the manner of relieving the outpost.

A. The new reserve marches to the post of the old one, where both rest with arms stacked, and the new commander receives from the old all information possessed by the latter in regard to the enemy, and the standing orders for the reserve. Each support marches to the post of the support which it is to relieve, and both supports rest, while information and orders are turned over as in the case of the reserves. When a new picket arrives to relieve an old one, each stands at ease while the new and the old commanders visit the sentinels' posts together, followed by the first relief from the new picket. The old commander points out to the new the important topographical features of the vicinity, and the known or suspected positions of the hostile posts; and gives him all the information that has been gained in regard to the enemy.

When the old sentinels and detached posts have been relieved, the commander of the old picket sends in a written report to the commander of the outpost or section, and (unless there appears to be danger of an attack) marches his picket back to its support. As soon as the support has been joined by its pickets, it marches back to its reserve, and the entire old outpost returns to camp; or each support may march directly back to camp as soon as it is joined by its pickets. If, while the old outpost, or any part of it, is returning, the enemy should attack, it must be at once marched back to the assistance of the new outpost.

Q. How often are outposts relieved?

A. As a rule, outposts should be relieved every twenty-four hours.

Q. If the army is on the march, when is the outpost relieved?

A. As soon as the advance guard has passed the chain of sentinels. The pickets will not, as a rule, fall back to the supports, but will join them at some designated point on the line of march, in order to save the fatigued men from unnecessary marching. The reserve follows the rear of the column, and the supports and pickets, united at designated rendezvous, form the rear guard of the column.

Q. If the army is retreating, what does the outpost form?

A. If the army is retreating, the outpost each day (when practicable) forms the rear guard.

CHAPTER V.

Reconnaissance.—Kinds of Patrols.

Q. What is the object of reconnaissance?

A. To gain a knowledge of the strength, position, and probable designs of the enemy, upon which the commander can base his own plans.

Q. Under what three heads may reconnaissance be considered?

A. 1. Reconnaissance in force;
2. Special reconnaissance;
3. Patrolling.

Q. By whose order, and how, is a reconnaissance in force made?

A. Only by the orders of the commander-in-chief, and the force employed generally consists of all three arms. They are often made just before an action, for the purpose of discovering the enemy's strength and dispositions, and frequently lead to a battle. The reconnaissance is conducted in the same general manner as a regular attack.

Q. What arms are especially valuable in reconnaissance in force, and why?

A. Cavalry and horse artillery are especially valuable in a reconnaissance in force, as they can be withdrawn from action more easily than infantry; and it would be well to limit the reconnaissance to these two arms when they are in ample force, and circumstances render their action sufficient. To be successful, however, a reconnaissance in force should impose upon the enemy the belief that he is encountering a real attack; and this consideration will determine the kind of troops to employ and the hour at which the attack should made. If infantry be employed in the attack, it will be hard to break off the action; but if it be not employed, it will generally be manifest that the attack is not serious.

Q. What are the advantages and disadvantages of making a reconnaissance in force in the evening, and what in the morning?

A. If it be made late in the afternoon, the troops may be withdrawn under cover of the darkness; but if made at that hour, the enemy will probably suspect the true nature of the operation. If made in the morning, the enemy will doubtless believe it to be a serious attack; but it may very easily precipitate a battle.

Q. To what three serious objections is a reconnaissance in force open?

A. 1. It often results in committing the troops so completely to action as to bring on a battle through the necessity of bringing up other troops to their assistance.

2. The withdrawal of the troops in pursuance to the general plan of the reconnaissance may often present the appearance of defeat, and thus injure the morale of the army.

3. It is always a costly means of gaining information.

Q. What is special reconnaisance?

A. Reconnaissances of this class have some limited and definite object in view: to discover whether a certain point is occupied in force by the enemy; whether a bridge is broken, or a defile is fortified; to capture a picket, with a view to gaining information; or to attack a post for the purpose of discovering the intentions or morale of the enemy.

Q. How is a special reconnaissance conducted?

A. It may be effected secretly, by a bold attack on a picket, by personal daring, or by any means which will carry out the object in view.

Q. How may a force employed on a special reconnaissance vary in size?

A. The force employed in a special reconnaissance varies in size from a company or troop to a division. The dividing line between a special reconnaissance and a reconnaissance in force is often very dim, and in many cases the same operation could be designated by either term.

Q. How are patrols primarily divided, and how does each vary in size?

A. Patrols are divided into *small* patrols and *strong* patrols. A strong patrol varies in strength from nine men to a troop of cavalry or a company of infantry. A small patrol varies from three men to a squad. A patrol should never consist of less than three men.

Q. Patrols are also classified as what kind? State briefly the duties of each.

A. They are also classified as *officers'*, *reconnoitering*, *visiting*, *covering* (flanking), and *connecting* patrols. To these may be added *exploring*, *harassing*, *expeditionary*, and *pursuing* patrols. The classification into small and strong patrols is the important one; for without changing its size, and without material modification of its methods, the patrol may combine the functions of several of the different kinds of patrols contained in the second classification. In fact, the latter classification is mainly for convenience of description.

Q. For what purpose are exploring patrols used?

A. To explore the region over which the troops are to operate. They report the condition of roads, railroads, bridges, rivers, woods, canals, telegraphs, villages, defiles, ponds and marshes, springs and rivulets, valleys, heights, etc.

Q. What should a patrol of any nature *always* do?

A. A patrol of any nature should endeavor to note carefully the different features of the ground over which it passes, whether required to make a report or not. *In every case a railroad embankment, a ditch, or any other object that would furnish a good defensive position, should be noted.* Good camping-places should also always be noted by exploring patrols.

Q. What are reconnoitering patrols?

A. *Reconnoitering patrols* are used to reconnoiter the position and watch the movements of the enemy.

Q. What are harassing patrols?

A. *Harassing patrols* are for the purpose of disturbing and annoying the enemy, and thus depriving him of sleep and rest.

Q. What are expeditionary patrols?

A. *Expeditionary patrols* have for their mission the capture of sentinels or patrols, or the destruction of roads, railroads, or telegraphs.

Q. What are connecting patrols?

A. *Connecting patrols* are used to preserve communication between columns of troops on the march or between different bodies in battle.

Q. What are pursuing patrols?

A. *Pursuing patrols* hang upon a retreating enemy, and render prompt information as to his movements, location, and morale.

Q. What is the size of the different kinds of patrols?

A. Exploring, reconnoitering, harassing, expeditionary, and pursuing patrols may be either strong or small; connecting patrols are always strong.

Q. What arm is generally best suited to patrolling, and why is the union of infantry and cavalry on this duty not desirable?

A. Cavalry is the best arm for patrolling. The composition of the patrol will, however, depend upon the ground to be reconnoitered, the distance to which the reconnaissance is to be extended, and the hour at which the patrol is sent out. Infantry is preferable to cavalry for patrolling only at night, or in a very close and broken country. It is often advisable to attach a few troopers to an infantry patrol merely as mounted orderlies, but no further union of the two arms on this service should ordinarily be contemplated. When bicyclists are with a command, they will, on good roads, be valuable for patrolling.

Q. What is the composition of a small infantry patrol?

A. Experienced soldiers should be detailed, and if no non-commissioned officer is available, an intelligent private should be selected to command the patrol, and the others ordered to obey him. It is desirable that at least one member of the patrol should be able to speak the language of the country in which the army is operating.

Q. How should the patrol be instructed?

A. The patrol commander should be given clear and definite instructions in regard to the object of the reconnaissance, what is known about the enemey, the nature of the ground to be reconnoitered, whether he is to reconnoiter in one direction or in several, how long he is to remain out, where his reports are to be sent, and, if other patrols are sent out at the same time, the particular route which he is to follow.

Q. How should the patrol be inspected?

A. The patrol commander inspects the patrol, being careful that each man has the proper amount of ammunition, and that none are sick, intoxicated, or foot-sore. He also sees that the arms and accouterments of his men are so arranged as neither to rattle nor glisten in the sunlight.

Q. How should the members of a patrol communicate with one another?

A. By signals, either those of the Drill Regulations, or any other found suitable; and by whistle.

Q. Every patrol should have what general formation?

A. The patrol should have the general formation of main body, advance guard, rear guard, and flankers, even when each can be represented by only one man. On nearing the enemy, the patrol should generally extend in line to facilitate observation. Figures 1 to 6, Plate 11, give typical formations of a small patrol.*

---

*It must be borne in mind that these typical formations are merely hints, the formation of the patrol always depending upon its object, the nature of the ground, and the character and position of the enemy.

PATROLS.

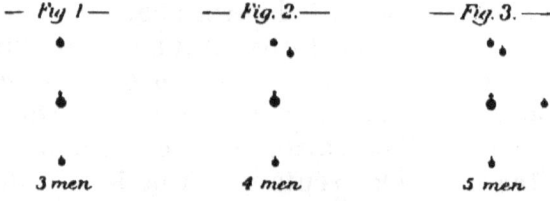

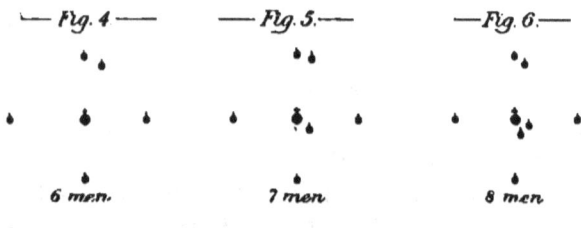

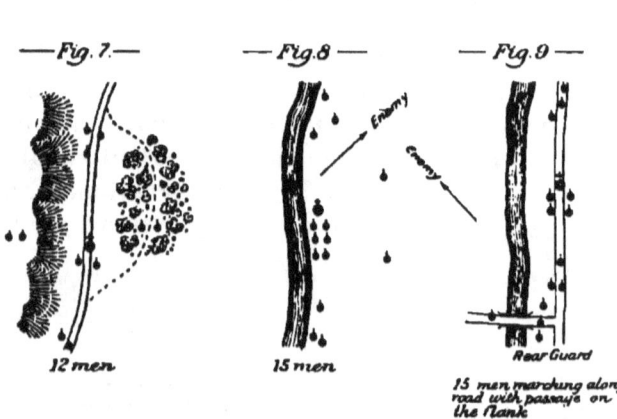

PLATE 11.

CHAPTER VI.

Duties of the Patrol.—Special Cases of Reconnoitering.

Q. What is the only definite rule that can be laid down for the formation of a patrol?

A. The only definite rule that can be laid down is the following: *The patrol must always be so formed as to facilitate the gaining of information, and to insure, if possible, the escape of at least one man, if the patrol should be cut off. Any disposition that complies with this rule is right.*

Q. What considerations influence the distances and intervals between the members of a patrol, and what are generally the minimum and maximum distances?

A. The distances and intervals depend upon circumstances. They are rarely less than twenty-five or more than one hundred yards. The men should be close enough to see and hear each other's signals, and for mutual support. On the other hand, they should not so crowd together that the patrol could not see more than a single man could.

Q. Of what should the point generally consist? how are the signals to and from the commander transmitted, and how is the patrol assembled?

A. The point should, when practicable, consist of two men, in order that one may scout vigilantly towards the enemy while the other watches for signals from the men on the right and left and from the commander. The signals from the other members of the patrol are generally transmitted to the commander through the point. To assemble the patrol, the commander signals to the point to halt, and moves up to it, followed by the rear guard man. The other men at once close in on the point, conforming their pace to that of the commander.

Q. How does the patrol move?

A. The patrol moves cautiously, *but not timidly*, along hedges, walls, ditches, ravines, etc., seeking in every way to see without being seen. It halts frequently to listen, and to make careful observation of the ground.

Q. How should a patrol generally return?

A. It is advisable for a patrol to return by a different route from the one followed on advance, if it be practicable for it to do so, as it thus extends its reconnaissance and lessens the danger of being cut off.

Q. What should the patrol do in regard to great roads?

A. Generally, the patrol should avoid moving on great roads and entering villages and inhabited places. But this does not mean that observation of great roads is to be neglected. On the contrary, they are the very ones that should be most carefully watched; for they are the routes that must be followed by any bodies of the enemy whose movements are really worth reporting. The patrol, while moving across fields and along such objects as have been already mentioned, should endeavor to keep a constant watch on the great roads. Inhabited places should be carefully observed, but should not ordinarily be entered by a small patrol. At night, or in a fog or snow-storm, the patrol must of necessity move on the great roads, in order to avoid losing its way, unless it is moving over ground with which it is perfectly familiar.

Duties of the Patrol.

Q. What is the general rule in regard to a patrol halting?

A. The patrol should not halt to rest before its return, unless circumstances render it imperatively necessary to do so. In such case it should rest in concealment in some place which offers advantages for defense, and from which a retreat can be easily effected.

Q. If another patrol of the same army or any friendly force is met, what should be done?

A. The patrol commander should exchange information with it, and inform himself of its strength, its destination, and the name of its commander, in order that he may report the same on his return.

Q. What should be done if a hostile patrol is discovered?

A. If a small hostile patrol is discovered, it is generally better to remain in concealment than to attack; for the noise of combat might cause enough mischief to more than counter-balance all that could be gained by defeating the hostile patrol, even if prisoners were captured. If the patrol is discovered by the hostile patrol, and finds itself unable to escape without fighting, it should attack boldly, and should endeavor to take prisoners. If the hostile patrol has penetrated so far as to make it probable that it has gained important information, an attempt should be made to ambuscade and capture it. If surprised, a patrol should fight resolutely, unless the enemy were in such force as to make resistance hopeless. In the later case, or if defeated in any case, the patrol should disperse, each man making his way back to the rendezvous designated beforehand. It should then, after uniting, continue its reconnaissance, sending one man back to the command with a report. It should be an invariable rule not to quit the reconnaissance until some result has been obtained.

Q. What should be done if the enemy is near at hand and in force?

A. If the enemy is near at hand and in force, the patrol must open fire, and keep up a lively fusillade in retreat, as the only means of giving prompt warning of impending danger.

Q. What should be done if the patrol falls into an ambuscade, and what if a hostile sentinel or patrol is suddenly encountered in the dark?

A. If, notwithstanding its prudence, the patrol falls into an ambuscade, it should boldly attack. If a sentinel or patrol of the enemy is suddenly encountered in the dark, no answer should be made to his challenge, but the patrol should remain halted and silent. The enemy may think himself mistaken and pay no further attention. If the challenge is repeated, the patrol should sneak away as quickly as possible, unless it has orders to capture prisoners, in which case a sudden rush upon the sentinel might enable the patrol to overpower him and carry him off before he could receive assistance. If some members of the patrol can speak the language of the sentinel, they may succeed in allaying his suspicions with a plausible answer to his challenge.

Q. What question should be asked of civilians coming from the direction of the enemy, or whose neighborhood has been visited by hostile troops?

A. Whenever the approach of people is signaled, the patrol remains concealed in observation. If they prove to be civilians coming from the direction of the enemy, they should be questioned carefully, as they may sometimes give valuable information. They should be asked whether they have seen any of the enemy's soldiers: where they were, what they were doing; whether they were infantry, cavalry, or artillery; whether they were regular troops or militia; what kind of uniforms they wore; whether the horses and men were in good condition, or seemed to be worn out and fatigued; how the troops of the enemy behaved themselves; how the road leading to the enemy is situated, and its condition; whether the enemy has scouting parties out; whether he seems to be vigilant; whether he has taken any guides from the village, etc.

Q. What should be avoided when questioning country people?

A. Questions formulating a statement to which the person questioned may answer "yes" or "no" should be avoided. The questions should be such as to draw out a narrative from the person interrogated.

Q. What precautions should be observed in questioning civilians?

A. It should always be borne in mind that the questions asked may be repeated to the enemy, and the questioner must, therefore, be careful so to frame them that they will not give a key to his own designs. When several persons are questioned, they should be examined separately.

Q. What should be done in regard to people going in the direction of the enemy?

A. They should be halted, and never allowed to proceed, unless they have undoubtedly genuine passes from proper authority.

Q. How should guides be selected and treated?

A. If it be necessary to take a guide from among the people of the country, he should be kindly treated, but warned that he will pay with his life the penalty of treachery. He must always be carefully guarded, and must not be discharged until there is no longer danger of his betraying the patrol. No one but the commander should communicate with the guides. Drovers, peddlers, livery-stable employees, and country doctors will generally be the best guides. If a man can be found who has served as a guide to the enemy, so much the better.

Q. What precautions are taken by the patrol with reference to concealment?

A. Whenever possible, the men composing the patrol should keep under cover.

Q. How are cross-roads reconnoitered?

A. When the patrol comes to a cross-road, two men should be sent along it on each flank until they come to the first turn, the patrol halting. If the men see nothing suspicious, they return, and the patrol pushes on. If anything suspicious is seen, one man rushes back quickly to the patrol, while the other remains in observation. If the patrol is very small, two men should be sent first to one side and then to the other, in preference to sending a single man in each direction.

Q. How is a height reconnoitered?

A. In reconnoitering a height, if the patrol is large enough to admit of detaching them, one or two men climb the slope on either flank, keeping in sight of the patrol if possible. In any case, one man moves cautiously up the hill, followed by the others in single file at such distance that each can keep his predecessor in view.

Q. How is a defile reconnoitered?

A. On approaching a defile, if time permits, the heights on either side should be reconnoitered by flankers before the patrol enters. If the heights are inaccessible, or time is urgent, the patrol pushes through, in single file, at double time, the distance being the same as in ascending a hill. The same method should be adopted in reconnoitering a railroad cut or sunken road.

Q. How is a bridge or ford reconnoitered?

A. At a bridge or ford, the front of the patrol is contracted so as to bring all men to the passage. The patrol then crosses rapidly, and takes up a proper formation. A bridge is first examined, to see that it is safe and has not been tampered with by the enemy.

Q. How are woods reconnoitered?

A. The patrol enters a wood in skirmishing order, the intervals being as great as may be consistent with mutual observation and support on the part of the members of the patrol. On arriving at the farther edge of the wood, the patrol should remain concealed and carefully look about before passing out to the open ground. When there is such a growth of underbrush as to make this method impracticable, a road through the wood must be reconnoitered as in the case of a defile, though not usually at double time. If in this case a cross-road is found in the wood, the patrol must be assembled and the lateral road reconnoitered before passing beyond it.

Q. How is an inclosure reconnoitered?

A. In reconnoitering an inclosure (such as a garden, park, or cemetery), the leading patrollers first examine the exterior, to make sure that the enemy is not concealed behind one of the faces of the inclosure. They then proceed to examine the interior. Great care should be taken in reconnoitering and entering an inclosure, as an imprudent patrol might find it a veritable trap.

Q. How is a house reconnoitered?

A. When a house or farm-building is approached by a patrol, it is first carefully reconnoitered from a distance, and if nothing suspicious is seen, it is then approached by two men, the rest of the party remaining concealed in observation. If the patrol is large enough to admit of it, four men approach the house, so as to examine the front and back entrances simultaneously. Only one man enters the door, the other remaining outside to give the alarm, should a party of the enemy be concealed in the house. The patrol should not remain in the vicinity of the house any longer than necessary, as information relative to its numbers and movements might be given to the enemy, if a hostile party should subsequently visit the place.

Q. How are villages reconnoitered?

A. If the village is seen to be in possession of the enemy, the patrol must be content with reconnoitering it from the outside. If the presence of the enemy is not apparent, the patrol should enter the village, being disposed in any way conforming to the general rule. A formation suitable in many cases would be in single file at proper distances for observation and support, each man being on the opposite side of the street from his predecessor. The patrol should push through the village as rapidly as possible; and when it has reached the opposite side, two of the party might be detached, if expedient, to reënter the village to seek further information, the rest of the patrol remaining in some position affording good observation and secure retreat.

If the patrol is strong enough, it should seize the postoffice, telegraph office, and railroad station, and secure all important papers that may be there. If the patrol is part of an advance guard, it should seize the mayor and postmaster of the place, and turn them over to the commander of the vanguard with the papers seized.

At night, a village must be even more cautiously approached by a small patrol than by day. The patrol should glide through back alleys, across gardens, etc., rather than move along the main street. If there are no signs of the enemy, they should make inquiry. If no light is seen, and it seems imprudent to rouse any of the people, the patrol must watch and capture one of the inhabitants, and get from him such information as he may possess.

The best time for a patrol to approach a village is at early dawn, when it is light enough to see, but before the inhabitants are up.

Q. How are cities and large towns reconnoitered?

A. As a rule, cities and large towns should not be entered by a small patrol, but should be merely watched from the outside.

CHAPTER VII.

Duties of the Patrol.—Indications of the Enemy.

Q. How is the reconnaissance of the enemy in position effected?

A. The patrol endeavors to ascertain the direction and extent of the line of observation, how its flanks are supported, the positions of the sentinels, their number, the number of pickets, the place where the line may be penetrated with the least risk of discovery, the strength of the hostile patrols, and the routes taken by them. It is also of great importance to ascertain whether good roads extend laterally behind the enemy's pickets, as such roads could be used by a force sent out to capture them. If the enemy's line of sentinels is penetrated, the patrol may, perhaps, approach near enough to the picket to overhear the countersign and parole; but it must be certain that the advantage to be gained is worth the risk, as the patrol will be in great danger of capture. If a point can be found on the flank of the enemy's position from which a view of his dispositions in rear of the line of sentinels can be obtained, the commander of the patrol endeavors to gain such point, and, concealing his patrol near at hand, makes careful observation. The best time for such observation is at daybreak, and the selected point should be gained before dawn, so as to enable the patrol to observe the relieving of the outpost. The longer the patrol remains, the more it will see, but the greater will be its danger of being discovered. The patrol commander should have sufficient courage to remain long enough to gain valuable information, and sufficient prudence to withdraw in time to escape capture.

If any important movements are observed, such as the withdrawing of the sentinels, the changing of their positions, preparations for advance or retreat, etc., the patrol commander sends a man back at once with a report of what has been seen.

Q. How is the reconnaissance of the enemy on the march effected?

A. If the enemy is on the march, the patrol should conceal itself close to the hostile column, but far enough away to escape discovery by the enemy's flankers. Conspicuous places should be avoided, even if at some distance from the column, as they would probably be carefully searched. The best place is a ditch or wallow, which will conceal the patrol and not be visible even at a short distance. The patrol carefully observes the progress of the column, noting its breadth of front, its rate of march, and the time it takes to pass a given point.

Q. How can the strength of a column be estimated?

A. A given point is passed in one minute by about 200 infantry in column of fours; by about 150 cavalry in fours at a walk, or, if in rear of the infantry, by about 100; by about 260 cavalry in fours at a trot, and by about 4 guns if in rear of infantry. If the whole column can be seen, and its length can be ascertained by the known distance between any two points which it passes, its strength can at once be estimated by allowing 1 yard for every 2 infantry soldiers, 1 yard for each cavalry soldier, and 20 yards for each gun or caisson. An allowance of from one-fourth to one-half must be made for opening out, depending upon the state of the roads and weather and the discipline of the troops composing the column.

Q. What indications are furnished by boats and bridges in the vicinity of the enemy?

A. If boats in great number are seen assembled on the bank of a stream, it is an indication of preparation to cross. If they are found burned, it is an indication of retreat. If important bridges are found broken, it is a sign of a long retreat. If at some distance above the point where we are preparing to throw a bridge, large boats heavily laden with stone are found, it is an evidence of the enemy's intention to destroy the bridge and oppose the crossing.

Q. What indications are furnished by the flames and smoke of the enemy's camp-fires?

A. If at night the flames of the enemy's camp-fires disappear and reappear, something is moving between the observer and the fires. If smoke as well as flame is visible, the fires are very near. If the fires are very numerous and lighted successively, and if soon after being lighted they go out, it is probable that the enemy is preparing a retreat and trying to deceive us. If the fires burn very brightly and clearly at a late hour, the enemy has probably gone, and has left a detachment to keep the fires burning. If, at an unusual time, much smoke is seen ascending from the enemy's camp, it is probable that he is engaged in cooking preparatory to moving off.

Q. What indications may be noted of the arrival and departure of troops?

Duties of the Patrol.

A. The rumbling of vehicles, cracking of whips, neighing of horses, braying of mules, and barking of dogs often indicate the arrival or departure of troops. If the noise remains in the same place, and new fires are lighted, it is probable that reinforcements have arrived. If the noise grows more indistinct, troops are probably withdrawing. If, added to this, the fires appear to be dying out, and the enemy seems to redouble the vigilance of his outposts, the indications of retreat are very strong.

Q. What characteristic noises are made by troops on the march, and at what distances can the various arms be heard?

A. The noise made by a strong column on the march is distinct and continuous; that of a small body, feeble and interrupted. The distance at which the noise of marching can be heard depends upon the nature of the ground marched over, the direction of the wind, and the presence or absence of other sounds. On a calm night, a company of infantry, marching at route step on a hard road, can be heard at a distance of 500 or 600 yards; a troop of cavalry at a walk, 600 or 700 yards; a troop of cavalry at a trot or gallop, artillery, and heavy wagons, 900 or 1000 yards.

Q. What indications are afforded by the dust raised by a marching column?

A. When infantry is marching, the dust is low and thick. With cavalry, the dust is higher; and as this arm moves rapidly, the upper part of the cloud is thinner and disappears more quickly than in the case of infantry. The clouds of dust raised by artillery and wagons are unequal in height and disconnected. Hence, by noting the length of a line of dust and the intervals in it, the strength and composition of the column may be estimated. The effect of the wind in dissipating the dust must, however, be taken into consideration.

Q. What indications are furnished by the reflection from the weapons of marching troops?

A. If the reflection is very brilliant, it is probable that the troops are marching towards the observer; otherwise, it is presumable that they are marching in the other direction.

Q. At what distance can various objects be seen, on a clear day, by a man with good vision?

A. At a distance of 9 to 12 miles, church spires and towers.

At a distance of 5 to 7 miles, windmills.

At a distance of 2 to $2\frac{1}{2}$ miles, chimneys of light color.

At a distance of 2000 yards, trunks of large trees.

At a distance of 1000 yards, single posts.

At 500 yards the panes of glass may be distinguished in a window.

Troops are visible at 2000 yards, at which distance a mounted man looks like a mere speck; at 1200 yards infantry can be distinguished from cavalry; at 1000 yards a line of men looks like a broad belt; at 600 yards the files of a squad can be counted, and at 400 yards the movements of the arms and legs can be plainly seen.

Q. What are some of the conditions which cause an object to look farther or nearer than it really is?

A. The larger, brighter, or better lighted an object is, the nearer it seems. An object seems nearer when it has a dark background than when it has a light one, and closer to the observer when the air is clear than when it is raining, snowing, foggy, or the atmosphere is filled with smoke. An object looks farther off when the observer is facing the sun than when he has his back to it. A smooth expanse of snow, grain fields, or water makes distances seem shorter than they really are.

Q. What information may be gained from the trail of the enemy?

A. If the ground is evenly trodden, the column was composed of infantry alone. If there are many prints of horseshoes, the column also contained cavalry. If the wheel tracks are deep and wide, artillery was in the column. If the trail is fresh, the column has recently passed. If the trail is narrow, the troops felt secure, as they were marching in column of route; if broad, they expected an action, as they were marching in column of platoons or companies, ready to deploy. If the fields on each side of the road are cut up with many tracks, the cavalry marched on the flanks of the column, and the enemy was pushing on with his troops well in hand for action. A retreating army makes a broad trail across fields, especially before the rear guard is formed and the retreat is regularly organized.

Q. What indications are furnished by an abandoned camp or bivouac?

A They are found mainly in the remains of campfires. These will show, by their degree of freshness, whether much or little time has elapsed since the enemy quitted the place, and the quantity of cinders will give an indication of the length of time he occupied it. They will also furnish a means of estimating his force approximately, ten men being allowed to each fire. Other valuable indications in regard to the length of time the position was occupied and the time when it was abandoned may be found in the evidences of care or haste in the construction of huts or shelters, and in the freshness of straw, grain, dung, or the entrails of slaughtered animals. Abandoned clothing, equipments, or harness will give a clue to the arms and regiments composing a retreating force. Dead horses lying about, broken weapons, discarded knapsacks, abandoned and broken-down wagons, etc., are indications of its fatigue and demoralization. Bloody bandages lying about, and many fresh graves, are evidences that the enemy is heavily burdened with wounded or sick.

Q. What inferences may be drawn from the manner and bearing of the inhabitants in a hostile country?

A. If the inhabitants are gloomy and anxious, it is an indication of a want of confidence in their cause, or that their troops are distant. If they are excited and insolent, it is an indication that their army is strong and near, and that they anticipate success. If they are friendly and pleasant in their demeanor, it is probable that the war is not popular, and that the Government lacks cordial support.

CHAPTER VIII.

Reports.—Special Patrols.—Cavalry Patrols.— The Cavalry Screen.

Q. When should reports be sent in, and what should be reported?

A. Reports should be sent in whenever anything of importance is seen, or anything happens which should be known to the officer who sent out the patrol.

Q. How should a verbal report be sent, and when are such reports better than written ones?

A. If a verbal report is sent in, it should be intrusted to an intelligent man, and he should be required to repeat it before starting, so as to be sure that he understands it. The man who carries the report should, if possible, himself deliver it to the officer for whom it is intended. If the country is dangerous and carefully watched by the enemy, the same report should be sent in by several men, each taking a different route. In this case a verbal report is better than a written one, as the enemy can not get possession of it by capturing the bearer, and the report of each man will be a check upon the accuracy of the others.

Q. What are the indispensable qualities of a written report?

A. Scrupulous accuracy as to facts, simplicity, clearness of diction, legibility of handwriting, and correct spelling of proper names. Surmises should never be given as facts, and the person making the report should carefully separate what he himself knows from what has been told him by others. Brevity is desirable, but not at the price of obscurity.

Sending Detachment	Location	Day	Mo.	Hrs. Min. a. m. or p. m.

Received,

To

Detachment No.   Report No.

Received   Hr.   Min.   M .... 189....

(Name)............................

(Rank)............................

Note.—A convenient form of report is given above.

Q. With what should the commander of the patrol be furnished?

A. If practicable, he should be furnished with a pad of printed report blanks. The receipt should be signed, torn off, and given to the bearer of the report as his voucher for its delivery. A report, either written or verbal, should invariably be made whenever the patrol returns.

Q. To what should the strength of a patrol be proportionate?

A. To the object to be effected by it. It should neither be so weak as to be obliged to retire before small parties of the enemy, nor so strong as to attract attention.

Q. What should always be specified, and with what should the patrol commander be provided?

A. The object for which the patrol is sent out should be distinctly specified, and the commander should be provided with a good map, by means of which he may select his route.

Q. What is the general nature of the formation of a strong infantry patrol?

A. The larger the patrol, the less secret are its movements, and the more nearly does its formation correspond to that of a column on the march, or a line deployed for action, as the case may be. As a rule, at least half the strength of the patrol should be in the main body; but its point, flanking, and rear groups each constitute a small patrol, and are each guided by the principles already laid down for the conduct of a small patrol, modified by their dependence on the main body.*

---

*Some typical formations of a strong patrol are given in the last three figures on Plate 11. Figures 7 and 8 explain themselves. In Figure 9 the men detached to reconnoiter and guard the bridge would ordinarily be sent out from the point, their places being taken, at double time, by men from the main body of the patrol. The patrol moves slowly, or halts if necessary, while the bridge is being reconnoitered. After the patrol has passed on, the detachment follows as rear group, the former rear group closing up to the main body of the patrol at double time. The detachment may in some cases be left to guard the bridge.

Q. How do the operations of an expeditionary patrol generally differ from a special reconnaissance?

A. Expeditionary patrols are generally strong patrols, although in some cases the object in view may be better attained by small ones. The object of an expeditionary patrol is always a special one, and the operations of a force of this kind generally differ from a special reconnaissance only in the size of the force employed.

Q. What is the most favorable moment for questioning prisoners, and why?

A. When they have just been captured. They are then agitated and have not sufficient self-control to deceive, and their answers at the place of capture may to a certain extent be verified. Such is not the case after the lapse of some time and in another place.

Q. By whom are the prisoners questioned?

A. By one of the officers of the detachment which captures them. Their replies are written down and transmitted with the prisoners to the Department of Intelligence, where they are questioned more at length.

Q. What is the relative value of different grades of prisoners?

A. It is more desirable to capture an officer than an enlisted man; an officer of high rank rather than a subaltern; a staff officer rather than a line officer. In brief, the object should be to capture those who are likely to possess the most extended information.

Q. If enlisted men are captured, what should they be questioned about?

A. They should be questioned in regard to their regiments, brigades, and divisions; the length of time they have been in the position; whether their rations are satisfactory; whether certain commanders are popular and have the confidence of their men; whether there are many men on sick report; what news has lately been received in camp, and what the rumors are —in brief, all questions calculated to elicit information in regard to the enemy's position, movements, and morale. If tact be exercised in questioning, much information may be gained; for the prisoner will probably consider the questions as prompted merely by natural curiosity.

Q. When the object is the destruction of roads, railroads, or telegraphs, or the tapping of a telegraph, how should the expeditionary patrol act?

A. When the object is the destruction of roads, railroads, or telegraphs, the expeditionary patrol should generally be a large one; but in some cases a small patrol may answer the purpose better, as it can move to its destination more secretly, and the use of high explosives gives it a great destructive power. In any case, the patrol should endeavor to reach its objective unseen, and part should be on the alert watching the enemy while the rest of the men are engaged in the work of destruction.

A patrol may be sent out to gain information by "tapping" a telegraph line. In this case, a telegraph operator, using a small pocket instrument, taps the line and learns the messages passing over it. The rest of the men, carefully concealed, look out for the enemy. An expeditionary patrol for the purpose of tapping a telegraph line is generally a cavalry patrol, sent out from the cavalry screen or from a raiding column.

Q. When may harassing patrols be used?

A. When an army halts in a position to await reinforcements, or because of the irresolution of its chief, the opposing commander (even if his army be inferior in numbers) may often raise the morale of his own troops, and impair the courage and efficiency of those of his adversary, by causing frequent alarms, destroying the enemy's rest; compelling the hostile outposts repeatedly to rush to arms, and exciting their sentinels to such a degree that they fancy a foe in every shadow, and imagine a hostile attack in every rustling leaf.

Q. Are harassing patrols small or strong?

A. They are generally strong; for, their object being not to seek information, but to annoy the enemy, they must be prepared to fight. In some cases, however, better results may be obtained by reducing the size and increasing the number of the patrols.

Q. What is the method of operating with a harassing patrol.

A. If the patrol is small, the enemy's sentinels should be shot down or captured in a noisy rush. If the patrol is large, the attack should be made upon the enemy's pickets; the object being the creation of alarm and the infliction of loss rather than the capture of prisoners. If many small harassing patrols are employed, strong patrols should be sent out, from time to time, to make vigorous attacks on the pickets; as the enemy would otherwise find it sufficient merely to redouble the vigilance of his sentinels and patrol to the front. The method of attack should be continually changed, and the point selected, the size of the assailing force, and the hour of attack should all be variable.

Q. What are the nature and duties of flank patrols?

A. They are always strong patrols, and usually operate on roads parallel to the line of march of the main body. They reconnoiter defiles, farms, woods, etc., at some distance from the flanks of the main column. They usually consist of from ten to twenty men (but may contain the maximum strength of a patrol), and are generally detached for a specific reconnaissance, with orders to rejoin the main body at a designated rendezvous, when the object of the reconnaissance has been gained. The patrol should avail itself of every practicable opportunity of communicating with the main column.

Q. When may flank patrols be called covering patrols?

A. Flanking patrols of the maximum strength are often detached from a marching column to reconnoiter and guard roads crossing the line of march during the passage of the main body. They are sometimes called *covering patrols*. The forces employed on this duty are, however, generally larger than patrols, and are covering detachments charged with the duties of a containing force.

Q. What are the essential differences between a cavalry and an infantry patrol?

A. Owing to the greater mobility of cavalry, the distances and intervals separating the scouts from each other and from the main body of the patrol are greater than in infantry. In very open country the cavalry scouts may sometimes be as far as 1000 yards apart. Another essential difference in the conduct of infantry and cavalry patrols, depending also upon the superior mobility of the latter, is the detaching of scouts from strong cavalry patrols. These scouts are not merely detached after the manner of the flankers, or even the flank patrols, of an advance guard; but work quite independently, joining the main body of the patrol at fixed rendezvous, or maintaining connection with it by occasionally sending in reports to its commander. These detached scouts usually work in pairs, one man being in command, and may be sent as far as five or six miles from the main body of the patrol. Each scout should understand what he is to look for, and how and where he is to make his report.

Q. What cavalry soldiers should be selected for patrol duty, and what is required in their inspection?

A. Intelligent and well-mounted soldiers. Before starting out, the patrol is carefully inspected by its commander, who, in addition to seeing that his men are in proper condition and properly equipped and supplied, assures himself that his horses are in good condition and well shod. The same precautions in regard to arms and accouterments are taken as in the case of an infantry patrol.

Q. What general rule may be prescribed for the formation of a cavalry patrol?

A. As in the case of infantry, no rules for the formation of the patrol can be positively prescribed, except the general and important one, that the patrol must always be so formed as to facilitate the gaining of information, and insure, if possible, the escape of at least one man if the patrol should be cut off.

Q. What are the distances and intervals between the different parts of a cavalry patrol?

A. The distances and intervals between different parts of a patrol depend upon circumstances. They should not be so great that the commander could not easily convey his commands by voice or signal, and would rarely exceed 100 yards except in open country. At night, the flankers and detached scouts should always be drawn in, unless their communication with the main body of the patrol is perfectly secured.

Q. How does a cavalry patrol conduct itself at night?

A. At night it must rely mainly upon its sense of hearing. Strict silence should be maintained, and smoking should be prohibited. Each scout should watch his horse for indications of danger, not only at night, but at all times; and if the animal pricks up his ears attentively or snorts excitedly, the warning should never be neglected, but the cause should be investigated.

Q. Why must a cavalry patrol move along good roads, and what precautions should it take?

A. Though exercising the utmost vigilance, and endeavoring to avoid being discovered, a cavalry patrol *must* move along good roads. To do otherwise would be to follow by-paths and traverse difficult ground, where the horses would often have to be led. The mobility which gives a cavalry patrol its special value would thus be lost, and the patrol would not be worth as much as one composed of infantry; for the horses would become a mere burden. The patrol should, however, always move upon soft ground or sward at the side of the road, if it be practicable to do so, and should always move with the least possible noise.

Q. In what details of the reconnaissance of different kinds of ground do the operations of a cavalry patrol differ from those of an infantry patrol?

A. The general manner of reconnoitering different

kinds of ground is the same as in the case of infantry patrols; but the following details should be noted: Scouts should peep around every corner or turn in the road before riding on. If they come to an object too extensive to be reconnoitered without assistance, they must signal for reinforcements, or one man must ride back and report to the patrol commander, while the others remain in observation. If obstacles are encountered on the road, such as barricades or felled trees, the patrol must, if possible, move round them and continue its reconnaissance. If the patrol can remove the obstacle, it does so; otherwise, or if a bridge is broken, word must be sent back, if a column is following.

In ascending a hill, a scout should not ride quite to the top; but, unless time is urgent, should halt at a short distance from the crest and then advance with caution. It may often be well for two scouts to approach the crest together, one of them dismounting and reconnoitering the crest on foot while the other holds his horse.

Q. If necessary to halt to feed or water, what places should be avoided, and what selected?

A. As a rule, a patrol should not halt at inhabited places, taverns, etc., or enter an inclosure. If it is necessary to halt to feed or water the horses, some secluded place should be selected, which could be guarded by sentinels in concealed positions.

Q. Of what are connecting patrols always composed, and how do they operate?

A. They are always composed of cavalry. They keep in the intervals between the different bodies, and detach scouts to the front and flanks. The scouts to the front watch the enemy; those on the flanks observe all movements and changes of position of the body of troops nearest them, with which they keep in constant communication.

Q. What are the composition and duties of pursuing patrols?

A. They are always composed of cavalry, and may be either small or strong. They keep on the trail of the enemy, do not lose contact with him, and keep their own army fully informed of his movements. They should have definite orders as to the distance to which they are to pursue, and the matters which it may be specially desirable to report. Pursuing patrols must not be confounded with a pursuing force following headlong upon the heels of a routed army to complete the destruction of battle. They merely follow, watch, and hang on an army that is retreating without demoralization, in order that touch with it may not be lost.

Q. What is an officer's patrol?

A. It is a patrol under the command of a commissioned officer, generally varying in strength from two to ten men. Sometimes it consists of one or two officers alone.

Q. How far does an officer's patrol ordinarily go from the command from which it is taken?

A. Generally not more than six miles; but it may be called upon to make very long and exhausting rides, and the men and horses should, therefore, be very carefully chosen. It may go very much farther than the ordinary scouting patrols, depending while gone entirely upon its own resources.

Q. When should a patrol sent out on a special mission return?

A. It should return the moment its object is accomplished, without undertaking other objects on its own responsibility. Care should be taken that neither too many missions nor too great an extent of ground be assigned to a single patrol.

Q. What precaution should the members of a patrol take in regard to papers on their persons?

A. They should not have on their persons any papers that could give information to the enemy. They should commit their orders to memory, and then destroy the printed or written copy.

Q. For what duty are officers' patrols especially valuable, and in entering a village or town what should they do?

A. Owing to the superior celerity and efficiency of officers' patrols, they are especially valuable in seizing postoffices, telegraph stations, etc. In entering a village or town in the enemy's country, the greatest safety is found in the sudden appearance and prompt disappearance of the party. The patrol should quickly gain the desired information, or seize the persons or documents constituting its object, and should disappear before the inhabitants recover from their astonishment sufficiently to appreciate how small, or how isolated, the party is.

Q. How is an army screened on the march?

A. By a veil of cavalry, which covers its movements, reconnoiters the enemy, and prevents him from gaining information in regard to the strength, dispositions, and designs of the force in rear.

Q. What is the distance of this screening force in advance of the main army?

A. As a rule, the screening force is at least one

march in advance of the main army. When the armies are concentrating, at the beginning of a campaign, the screening force may sometimes be pushed many miles ahead; but when the armies begin their advance, the distance is usually reduced to not more than fifteen or twenty miles, diminishing on contact to five or six, and finally disappearing altogether when tactical operations begin—the veil then separating, and uncovering the front of the army.

Q. How is the front of each army corps on the march covered?

A. As a rule, the front of each army corps on the march is covered by a brigade of cavalry, the front of the cavalry brigade on screening duty averaging ten or twelve miles. When the brigade constituting the cavalry screen is operating in an open country, one regiment constitutes the reserve, and is preceded by a squadron of each of the other regiments at a distance of about two and a half miles. These squadrons, constituting the supports, are separated by an interval of not more than six miles, the reserve being situated centrally in their rear. About two and a half miles farther to the front is the second squadron of each advanced regiment, either in one column, or in two columns of two troops each. These are termed the intermediate squadrons. They are separated by about the same interval as the squadrons composing the supports. About two and a half miles farther to the front, the remaining squadron of each regiment is distributed along the front in contact troops, which are preceded at suitable distances by patrols, detailed either from the contact troops, the intermediate squadrons, or the supports. When necessary, these patrols detach scouts still farther to the front. This formation may be modified in many ways; the great requirement of the formation of the screen being that it should be able to get information of the enemy and prevent him from getting information in turn. On gaining contact with the enemy, the cavalry forming the screen should concentrate to fight; for the best way to screen an army is by defeating and driving away the opposing cavalry.

Q. State the miles regulating the conduct of the cavalry screen.

A. The following rules regulate the conduct of the cavalry screen:

1. Explore the country well to the front with small patrols, which must not lose contact with the enemy.

2. Keep the supporting bodies well in hand, so as to be able to concentrate rapidly.

3. Always maintain a reserve when near the enemy.

4. Keep up constant communication between all parts of the screen and with the troops in rear.

5. Always form and maneuver the screen with a view to beating the opposing cavalry. This is the paramount consideration.

CHAPTER IX.

Rear Guards.

Q. How is the withdrawal of a defeated army covered on the field of battle, and when does the duty of the rear guard begin?

A. On the field itself the withdrawal is covered by the artillery and cavalry, especially the latter when the ground favors its action; and it is only when the first halt is effected that the rear guard can be organized and a regular retreat begun.

Q. Why is it that a retreating army can be protected by a fraction of itself?

Q. Because the enemy must change from order of battle to order of march to pursue, and he can at first bring only the heads of his columns against the rear of the retreating force.

Q. Why must a rear guard be organized as soon as possible?

A. The rear guard must be organized as soon as possible, even at the expense of a delay comparatively near the enemy; for to trust to speed entirely in escaping would be to make such long and continued forced marches as to ruin the efficiency of the army and disintegrate it by straggling.

Q. By what must the rear guard profit, and what two courses of action are then open to the enemy's choice?

A. The rear guard must profit to the utmost by the defensive features of the ground, and at every opportunity take up a defensive position. The enemy will then have but two courses of action open to his choice: either to attack with the heads of his columns, or to deploy for action. In the former, his advanced troops should be easily repulsed; in the latter, he will be compelled to lose time in deploying, while the rear guard (which should wait until the enemy's dispositions for attack are about completed) should quickly ploy and disappear from his front, only to repeat the operation at the next favorable ground. In the meantime, the enemy, unable to advance quickly in deployed lines, again loses time in changing to a marching formation, and the main body of the retreating army steadily continues on its way without halting.

Q. What is the strength of the rear guard under various conditions, and what are the objections to having it too large or too small?

A. The strength of the rear guard depends upon the nature of the country, and the strength and character of the pursuing force. In a broken country full of good defensive positions, it would be less than in an open country; and it would be greater when the pursuit was vigorously pushed in force than when it was feebly conducted by small parties. As a rule, it corresponds to the strength of an advance guard on a forward march; and would, consequently, vary from one-eighth to one-third of the entire force—generally consisting of about one-sixth. Care and good judgment are necessary in determining the strength of the rear guard. If it were too large, too many troops would be kept upon a peculiarly trying duty, and the object of the commander to withdraw quickly as many men as possible to a place of safety would be thwarted. If it were too small, it would be continually driven in upon the main body, to which it would communicate alarm and confusion; and the latter might even be compelled to halt and fight for the protection of the rear guard.

Q. What troops should be selected for the rear guard, and what should be done to raise their morale?

A. The best troops should be selected; generally those which have suffered least in the battle, or which have gained therein some local success; and their morale should be still further raised, if practicable, by occasional ambuscades or offensive returns against the enemy, whenever an opportunity of taking him at a disadvantage occurs.

Q. When, and how, should offensive returns be made?

A. They are generally made when the rear guard is closely pressed by the enemy at a bridge, defile, or ford. They should not be pushed far; for their result, at best, can only be a moral one, and the distance between the main body and the rear guard must not be dangerously increased.

Q. What qualities should be possessed by the commander of the rear guard, and (briefly) how should he conduct its operations?

A. He should be as prudent as a man can be without being timid, and as brave as a man can be without being rash. He should constantly present a bold front to the enemy, and should ever be ready to fight, even to the extent of sacrificing himself and his entire command if necessary; but he should remember that the great duty of the rear guard is to gain time, and he should know when to withdraw. He should be able to distinguish the enemy's preparations for a serious attack from insignificant demonstrations, and he should never allow the enemy to force him into a fight contrary to his own interests and intentions. He should never expect assistance, and should feel disgraced if the main body should be obliged to suspend its retreat to come to his aid.

Q. In general terms, what is the distance of the main body from the rear guard, and what are the objections to having it too great or too small?

A. In general terms, it may be said to be usually about the same as that of the advance guard from the main body on advance. If the distance were too great, the rear guard would be in danger of being cut off; if the distance were too small, the main body would be subject to constant alarms, and each reverse of the rear guard would quickly affect the main body, whose retreat would be constantly harassed by the enemy.

Q. What is the formation of the rear guard?

A. It is that of an advance guard reversed. Nearest the main body is the reserve, after which follow the support and the rear party, the extreme rear being composed of a point. The distances between the various bodies composing the rear guard are the same as those between the corresponding bodies of the advance guard. Flankers are thrown out as in the case of an advance guard, but they are more numerous, and the line joining them is a more pronounced curve, for the reason that flank attacks are more to be feared than in the case of an advance guard, and the flanks must, therefore, be more carefully covered.

Q. Of what arms should the rear guard be composed?

A. The composition of a rear guard is practically the same as that of an advance guard. It is generally composed of all three arms; but if there are enough cavalry and horse artillery to admit of the rear guard being composed exclusively of those arms, it would be best, except in a very close and rugged country, to leave the infantry with the main body.

Q. How many guns should there be with the rear guard, and what may their effective use do?

A. There should be as many guns with the rear guard as can be effectively used and freely maneuvered. The effective use of artillery may obviate the necessity of deploying the other arms of the rear guard, the deployment of the enemy at a distance being compelled by the fire of the guns.

Q. How should the artillery of the rear guard be used, and what should be done if it becomes necessary to abandon the guns?

A. The fire of the artillery at short range should be as rapid as is compatible with its cool and intelligent action. If it becomes necessary to abandon the guns, the equipments and breech-blocks should be carried away, and, if there seems to be no hope of recovering the lost pieces, the guns should be burst and the caissons blown up. The danger of losing a few guns must never be made an excuse for a premature withdrawal.

Q. How should cavalry be used with the rear guard?

A. The cavalry of the rear guard can charge bodies of the enemy that have been thrown into confusion by the ardor of pursuit, or by the fire of the artillery; but its chief reliance should be in dismounted fire-action.

Q. How are the several arms arranged in a rear guard composed of all arms?

A. The infantry should be with the reserve, and the cavalry with the support and rear party. If the cavalry is not in sufficient strength for the entire support, the deficiency must, of course, be made up from the infantry. The artillery should be with the reserve; but horse artillery may sometimes accompany the support. The engineers should be at the rear of the reserve or at the head of the support. Machine-guns may be used with effect by the rear guard. They should generally be with the support.

Q. How may a rear guard be described?

A. As a reversed advance guard with more flankers. (See Plates 12 and 13.)

Q. How is the withdrawal of the rear guard from action executed?

A. The manner of withdrawing a rear guard from action will depend entirely upon circumstances. As a rule, only a portion should withdraw at a time, taking up, if necessary, a new position, to cover the withdrawal of the rest. The guns especially must not all withdraw at once, as the total cessation of artillery fire would betray the movement. Whether the withdrawal should be by alternate battalions, or whether it should begin at the center or at a flank, would depend upon the direction and progress of the attack and the topography of the field. Generally, the infantry and a portion of the guns withdraw first; and when they are again in position or *en route*, they are followed by the remaining guns and the cavalry.

Q. What precautions should be taken to insure the right road being followed by the rear guard?

A. Uninterrupted communication must be maintained between the several parts of the rear guard and

Rear Guards. 187

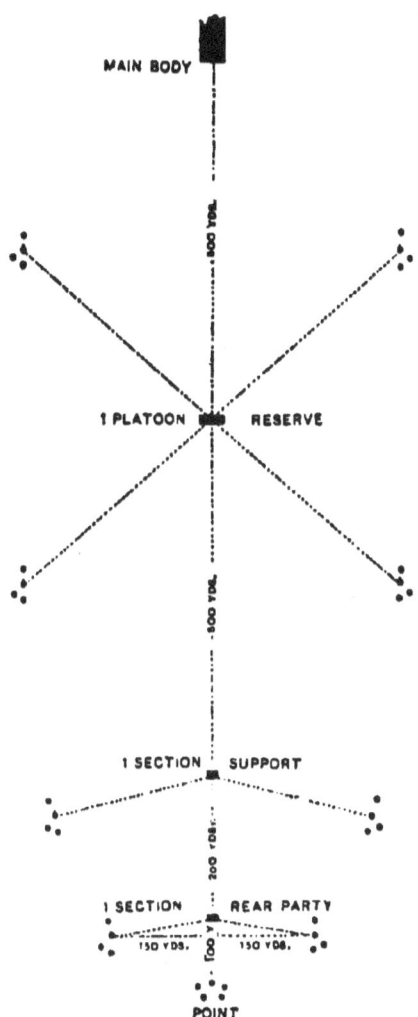

PLATE 12.

188 *Elements of Military Science.*

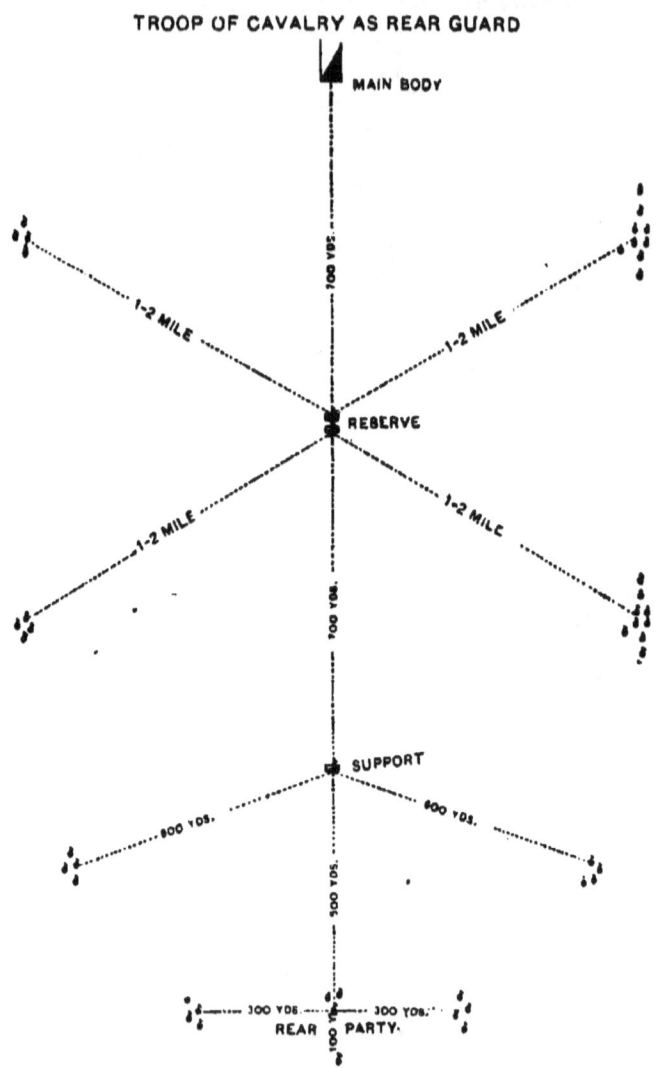

PLATE 13.

the main body. The road should be carefully marked, so that the rear guard may not lose its way.

Q. Why must the flanks of a rear guard be guarded with especial care, and what provision is made for protecting them from surprise?

A. Patrolling must be carried on with vigilance and energy, especially on the flanks. The enemy, finding a firm front opposed to all his direct attacks, will undoubtedly attempt to cut in on the flanks, where, in fact, always lie his most promising hopes of success; for if he can cause the rear guard to form front to a flank, any assault by which it can be pushed off the road will uncover the rear of the main body, and will be only less disastrous to the retreating army than the destruction of the rear guard itself. Prompt notification of attempts against the flanks should be given by the patrols (who are often warned of them by a diminution of the enemy's forces following in rear), and the rear guard should then endeavor with celerity to slip past the menaced point; failing in this, it should form a strong front towards the attacking force.

Q. If the two armies are of approximately equal strength, why should the rear guard have, at first, an advantage over the opposing advance guard; and why does not this advantage continue?

A. If two armies are of approximately equal strength, the rear guard will be about as stong as the advance guard of the force pursuing it, and the advantage of a good defensive position should give it a superiority over the latter. But this superiority will be only temporary at best; for the advance guard is receiving constant accessions of strength from the rear, while the distance between the rear guard and the main body of the retreating force is constantly increasing.

Q. In regard to what is the pursuing army always in doubt?

A. The pursuing army will always be in more or less doubt as to the strength of the force which it finds barring its way, and it must act with prudence, or run the risk of a serious and costly repulse. The morale of the retreating force is also a matter of uncertainty to the pursuers, and this consideration also forbids rash action.

Q. What advantage has the rear guard over the pursuing force in regard to the ground?

A. It is not obliged to reconnoiter the ground over which it has to march. All necessary information as to the roads is furnished from the front, and a well-qualified staff-officer with the main body should select defensive positions for the rear guard, and furnish its commander with a description (and, if possible, a topographical sketch) of the same. The positions would be ridges, sunken roads, villages, woods, bridges, or defiles.

Q. When should the rear guard make use of defensive positions?

A. When it is essential that the army should put distance between itself and the enemy, the rear guard must make use of every good defensive position to delay the pursuers; but no halt should be made for fighting when the necessity of checking the enemy and gaining time is not imperative.

Q. How long should the rear guard occupy a defensive position?

A. The rear guard must not be tempted by the great natural strength of a position to occupy it at the expense of being separated at too great a distance from the main body, nor to hold it so long as to become compromised in a regular engagement. The amount of resistance to be made by the rear guard will depend upon the judgment of its commander, or on the orders of the commander-in-chief.

Q. To what extent should the commander-in-chief supervise the operations of the rear guard?

A. At very important positions, he should join the rear guard, if necessary, superintending its formation for resistance, or even conducting its action. It is best, however, never to interfere with the commander of the rear guard, if he understands his business and performs his part properly. The nature of his duty requires that he should have even greater independence of action than the commander of an advance guard.

Q. Why do defiles offer good opportunities to an energetic pursuer and to an able rear guard commander?

A. To the former they afford a chance of cutting off the rear guard by interposing a force at the entrance of the defile. To the latter they afford a double opportunity of administering a check to the enemy, who is compelled to narrow his front.

Q. How may a defile be defended at the entrance?

A. If practicable, the position at the entrance of the defile should be convex towards the enemy, so as to admit of ready withdrawal by the flanks. In defending a defile, the main body leaves a detachment to hold the heights on each side until relieved by the infantry of the rear guard. The artillery is generally stationed at the entrance of the defile, and the cavalry in the best position for dismounted fire-action—always at that part of the line which is to withdraw last. As soon as the enemy has not only deployed for attack, but is well committed to the assault, the artillery fires its parting round of shrapnel, and withdraws rapidly through the defile, followed by the infantry. The cavalry covers the withdrawal of the other arms, mounting at the last moment, and retreating rapidly through the defile, its retreat being protected, if practicable, by infantry skirmishers lining the crest on either side of the interior of the defile.

Q. How may a defile be defended at the outlet?

A. The outlet of the defile always affords a better position for opposing the enemy than the entrance; for in making a stand with a defile at its back, the rear guard runs the risk, in case its flank is turned, of being cut off altogether. In making a stand at the farther side, the artillery is posted so as to rake the defile; and the infantry, so as to bring a converging fire on its outlet, detachments of infantry also holding the crest; while the cavalry is stationed so as to be able to charge the enemy in flank as he emerges from the defile. Enough of the enemy should be allowed to pass to enable the assault upon him to be more than a mere stroke at the head of his column; but the mistake of allowing too many to pass would be a fatal blunder. Here the judgment of the rear guard commander must come into play, and no rule or suggestion can aid him. The enemy having been severely handled and thrown back into the defile, the rear guard withdraws without delay.

Q. Besides fighting, what measures should be taken by the rear guard?

A. All measures to impede his progress by blocking his path, destroying bridges, etc.

Q. How may villages be utilized by a rear guard?

A. They may be fortified in some cases, but generally it will be more expedient to burn them, and thus place a barricade of fire, so to speak, between the rear guard and the enemy; but this measure will, manifestly, be of value only when the enemy is following close upon the heels of the rear guard.

Q. What should always be resorted to by the rear guard?

A. Any means of producing suffering and inconvenience to the pursuers, such as to cause them to delay, should be resorted to by the rear guard, stopping only at such measures as are condemned by the laws of war.

Q. Are these negative measures sufficient in themselves?

A. No. They are merely helps, and the safety of the retreating force must depend upon the resolute action of the rear guard itself.

Q. What should be done with stragglers, and with the sick and wounded, with the rear guard?

A. The rear guard should collect all stragglers and compel them to move on, and it should not allow the sick or wounded to be left behind, unless they prove a dangerous encumbrance.

Q. At each halt, what is done by the rear guard?

A. It chooses a good defensive position, and establishes its outposts towards the enemy.

Q. When an army is retreating by several parallel roads, how are the rear guards formed and commanded?

A. Each column will then have its own rear guard, each rear guard having its own chief, and all being united, when practicable, under the command of one common superior. Connection should be maintained between the several columns, and between the different rear guards, by connecting groups or patrols.

Q. What are the duties of the rear guard on a forward march?

A. The rear guard should never begin its march until all the baggage has moved off. The provost-marshal and provost guard generally march with the rear guard, which takes charge of all prisoners arrested by them. If marching in a hostile country, the rear guard is charged with the protection of the baggage from the forays of guerillas, and if the country is suited to partisan warfare, and the enemy's raiding parties are enterprising, its duty greatly increases in importance. It should carefully watch the flanks of the baggage train with patrols, of a number and size suited to the danger to be apprehended, and should be ready to repel attacks on the flanks as well as on the rear of the train.

PART III.

Field Fortification.—Marches.—Supply.

CHAPTER I.

Field Fortification.

Q. What is the object of all fortification?

A. So to strengthen a position that the forces occupying it may successfully resist or subdue their adversaries.

Q. Into what two classes is fortification divided?

A. Into Permanent, and Temporary or Field Fortification.

Q. What are the subdivisions of field fortification?

A. First, Hasty Intrenchments, by which an army in the presence of the enemy seeks to protect itself from the direct effect of his fire. Second, Field Works, for the temporary protection of important points, such as cities, arsenals, bridges, fords, and of military positions in general. Third, Siege Works, for the reduction of fortified positions. These will not be considered in this work.

Q. Why are hasty intrenchments indispensable to-day, and of what do they consist?

A. The intensity of fire of modern small arms makes some sort of protection absolutely necessary, and this protection can in the general case be furnished only by hasty intrenchments. These consist ordinarily of parapets of earth hastily thrown up, whence their name. The parapet with its trench constitutes the shelter trench, so called. All hasty intrenchments are of three types, according as the line protected is lying down, kneeling, or standing. The last two require, of course, more time in construction that the first, and are resorted to only when the position is to be occupied for a comparatively long time. (See Plate 14.)

The principal function of the shelter trench, as already stated, is to shelter infantry, and to protect it against the fire of the enemy's infantry. So important is it now to have the protection of the shelter trench that all infantry troops carry intrenching tools as an integral part of their equipment.

Q. On what does the location of trenches depend?

A. Primarily, on tactical considerations; and secondarily, on the nature of the ground.

Q. What conditions should always be satisfied by shelter trenches?

A. While affording the most complete cover possible under the circumstances, they should have a free field of fire to the front, and should not interfere with or hinder the quick resumption of the offensive.

Q. How is cover for guns and caissons obtained?

A. Either by sinking the gun below the surface of the ground and building a parapet with the excavated earth, or by leaving the gun on the natural surface of the ground and building an epaulment in front and on the flanks. The first construction is called a gun-pit; the second, a gun epaulment.

Q. When are field works employed?

A. When a position is to be held for a considerable period, and time is available.

Q. What special conditions must field works satisfy?

A. 1. They must afford protection against both rifle and artillery fire.

2. They must be of suitable size for the garrison that is to occupy them.

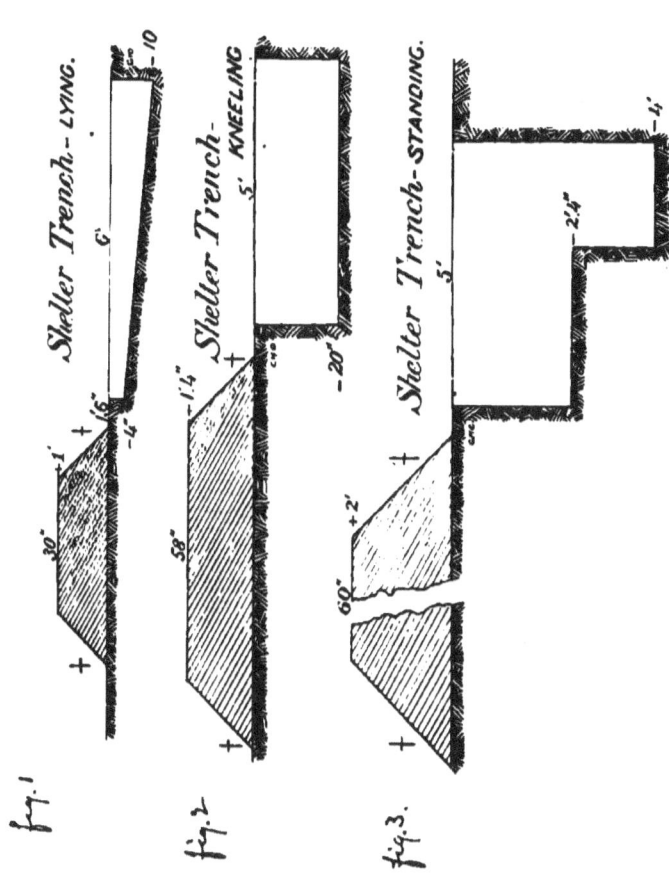

PLATE 14.

3. They should have suitably constructed casemates to shelter the garrison by night.

Q. Define parapet, trace, and profile, and give the names of the various parts of the profile.

A. A parapet is a bank of earth thrown up to cover the defenders while firing; the trace of a work is its outline in plan, though the term is frequently applied to the horizontal projection of its interior crest. (See Plate 15, Figure 1.) The profile is a cross-section of the work made by a plane perpendicular to the interior crest. (See Plate 15, Figure 2.)

In the profile, the various parts have received the following names:

(a) banquette slope, (g) scarp,
(b) banquette tread, (h) counterscarp,
(c) interior slope, (D) ditch,
(d) superior slope, (i) interior slope of glacis,
(e) exterior slope, (k) glacis,
(f) berm, (t) trench.

The intersection of the superior and of the interior slopes is called the interior crest; that of the superior and of the exterior, the exterior crest. The thickness of the parapet is the horizontal distance between these two crests.

Q. What is meant by a traverse? by an embrasure? by the command of a work and its relief? by the terreplein?

A. A traverse is a bank of earth inside a work to protect some part of it from direct fire. Usually they are set at right angles to the interior crest of the parapet, to protect the latter from enfilade. An embrasure is a revetted opening in the parapet, through which field guns may fire. The command of a work is the

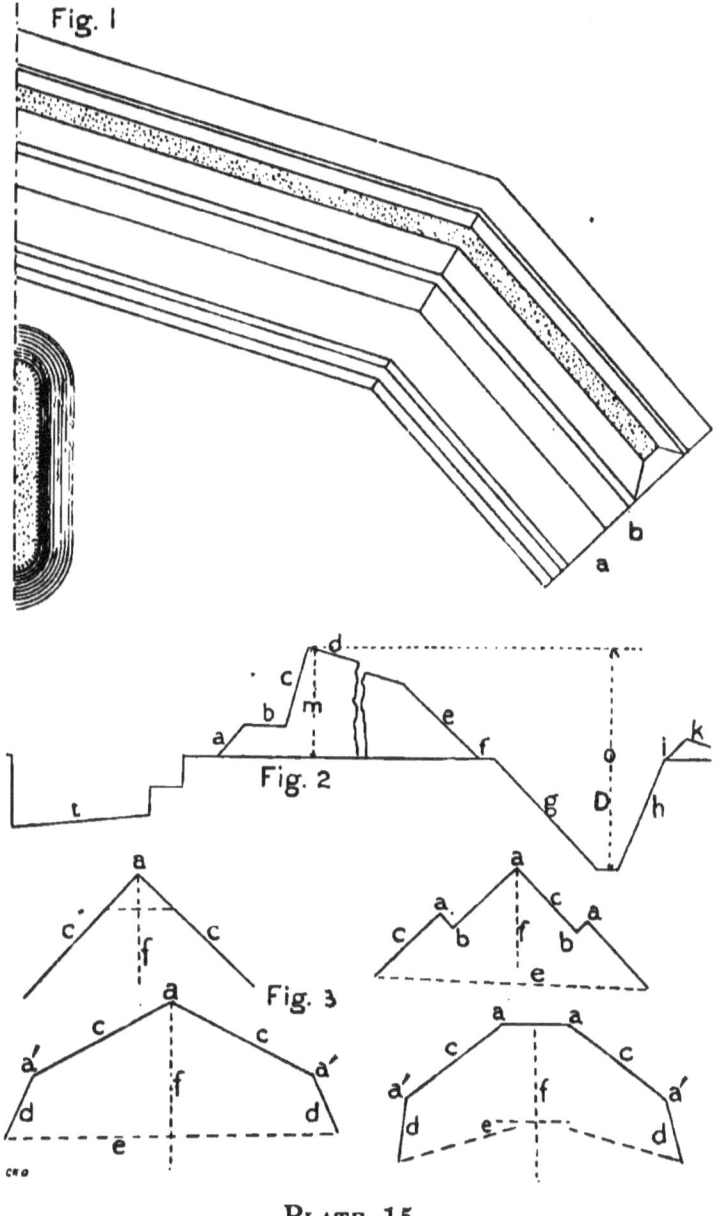

PLATE 15.

height of its interior crest above the ground on which it is constructed (*m*, Figure 2, Plate 15). Its relief is the height above the bottom of the ditch (*o*, Figure 2, Plate 15). The terreplein is the surface of the ground inside the work.

Q. How, if possible, should the glacis lie with respect to the superior slope?

A. It should be parallel to the superior slope, in order to get the best fire-effect from the position.

Q. Point out (Plate 15, Figure 3) the elements of a work with respect to the trace.

A. With respect to the traces of various works,

a is a salient angle,   *c, c, c* are faces,
a' is a shoulder angle,   *d, d, d* are flanks,
b is a reëntrant angle,   *e, e* is the gorge,
f is the capital.

Q. How are field works classified?

A. Field works are classified with reference to their trace, as:

(a) Open—*i. e.*, having thick parapets on the exposed sides, the rear or gorge being open;

(b) Closed, in which the parapet is continuous;

(c) Half-closed, which differ from the open in that the gorge is closed by obstacles, stockade work, or shelter trenches.

Open works have the advantage over closed, of affording greater freedom of movement to the defenders, and in the event of capture, of being exposed to fire and assault from the works in rear. Closed works, while affording greater protection from assault, are liable to have their parapets exposed to enfilade or to reverse fire; besides which, the available interior space is much reduced.

Field Fortification.

Q. What is the difference between a fort and a redoubt?

A. A fort has reëntering angles, while a redoubt has none. A fort can thus sweep its own ditches by fire from its own parapets, but a redoubt cannot. From another point of view, redoubts are of much simpler trace than forts, and are therefore more easily built.

Q. Explain what is meant by "sector of fire," "dead space."

A. By "sector of fire" is meant the angular space in front of a work that is swept by its own fire; the limiting space is usually taken at 60 degrees, being 30 degrees on each side of a perpendicular to the parapet over which the fire is delivered. Such parts of the terrain in front of a parapet as cannot be reached by fire from the parapet itself constitute what is called "dead space," or "undefended space." Thus, in the case of a salient of 60 degrees, there would evidently be a dead space of 60 degrees. (Plate 16, Figure 1.)

In Figure 2, Plate 15, the angular space e, f, g, h, i, k is called the "dead angle," because it cannot be reached by fire from the parapet. Both dead space and dead angle diminish the offensive value of a work, and have to be corrected by flanking arrangements from neighboring works, or by such an alteration of the trace of the work itself as to provide a fire sweeping the ditches and the dead spaces.

Q. How may the defensive power of field fortifications be increased?

A. By the use of obstacles. These have for their object the holding of the enemy under fire while checking his advance and breaking up his formation.

204   *Elements of Military Science.*

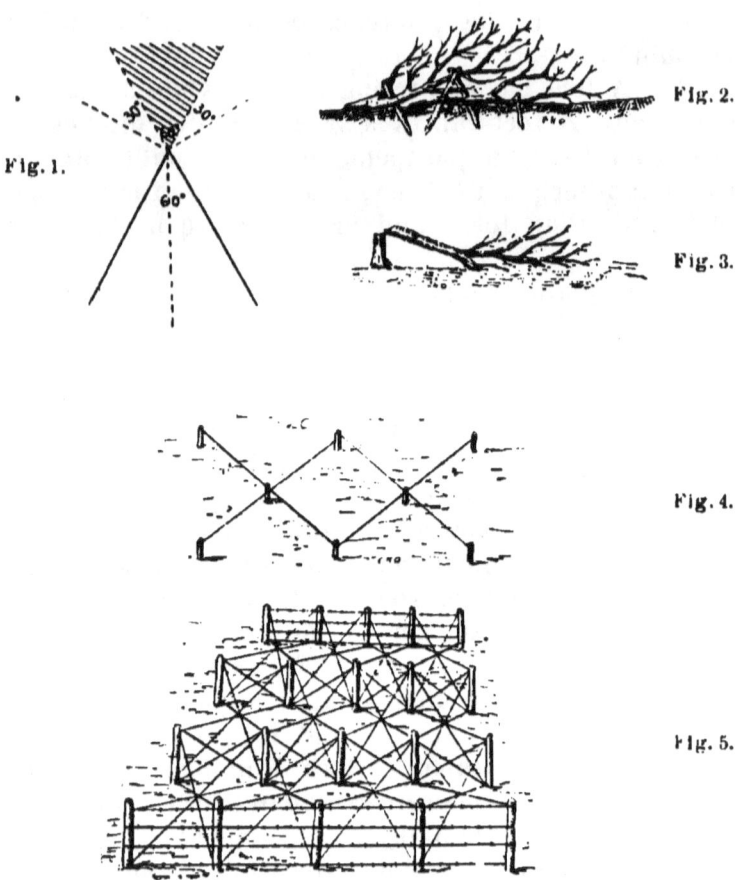

Fig. 1.

Fig. 2.

Fig. 3.

Fig. 4.

Fig. 5.

PLATE 16.

Field Fortification.

Q. What conditions should all obstacles satisfy?

A. 1. They must be within the effective zone of the defenders' fire, and must be so arranged as to offer the least obstacle possible to the advance from the side of the defense.

2. They must be concealed as far as possible from the view of the assaulting party, so that this may come upon them as a surprise.

3. They must be difficult of removal under fire, and, if possible, should be of such construction as will necessitate the use of tools not usually carried by troops.

4. They should, if possible, be so placed as to be secure from the fire of the enemy's artillery, and so constructed that, if struck by his projectiles, they will suffer small damage.

5. They must offer no shelter to the enemy.

Q. What form of obstacle is most commonly used?

A. The abatis. This consists of branches of trees about 15 feet long laid on the ground, butts to the rear, all small twigs being cut off, and all large branches pointed and interlaced. The abatis should be 5 feet high. The branches are secured to the ground by forks, wire, or by logs laid over the butts of the branches. (Plate 16, Figure 2.)

The abatis most easy of construction is that made by felling trees toward the enemy, in such manner as to leave the fallen part still attached to the stump, the branches being then pointed as already described. (Plate 16, Figure 3.)

Q. What are wire entanglements, and how are they constructed?

A. These are obstacles consisting of wire wound between stakes about 18 inches long, driven into the ground about 6 feet apart. The ground should not be cleared, as bushes, etc., increase the delaying effect of the entanglement. The entanglement (Plate 16, Figure 4) just described is called a low wire entanglement. The high wire entanglement is constructed in the same manner, except that the stakes are at least 4 feet long and are driven from 6 to 8 feet apart, the wire leading from the head of the stake to the foot of the one diagonally opposite. The line of stakes in front and in rear should, if possible, be finished off like fencing, with barbed wire; the use of this is not recommended for the interior cross-work, on account of the difficulty of handling it, and of the great length of time consequently necessary. (Plate 16, Figure 5.)

Q. What are palisades, and when are they used to most advantage?

A. Palisades consist of rows of trunks of trees or of squared trunks, 8 or 10 feet high, planted close together, and pointed on top. When material is at hand, ribband pieces should be spiked on the inside along their tops about a foot or two below the points, in order to steady the row. Palisades are used to great advantage in the bottoms of ditches or to close the gorges of field works.

CHAPTER II.

MARCHES AND SUPPLY.

Marches.

Q. Why is marching so important in a military point of view?

A. Because the march is the foundation of all operations, and upon its proper performance depends the success of all military undertakings.

Q. What considerations govern marches executed, first, at a distance from the enemy; second, within striking distance of him?

A. In the first case, the comfort and convenience of the men must be promoted by all possible means; in the second, all considerations of comfort must yield to the necessity of securing one's self against unexpected attack, and to that of being constantly in readiness for combat.

Q. How should a large force be subdivided for a march?

A. Into as many columns as there are roads approximately parallel to the direction of march; these columns should take up as broad a front as possible, provided that they are not too far apart for easy communication, and for ready support one of the other. A division composed of all arms can with ease be formed in one column. In general, the march of a large force in a single column is attended with disadvantages, but in the movement of the vast armies of modern times, it will seldom be possible to assign less than an army corps to one road.

Q. Upon what does the number of columns into which a force is divided for marching depend?

A. Partly upon the number of main roads existing in the zone of march, partly on the distance of the enemy, and partly on the immediate object in view.

Q. On what does the marching formation of troops depend?

A. Chiefly on the breadth of the road. A main road may admit of infantry marching 6 or 8 abreast, and of two carriages side by side. Cavalry and horse artillery should not march on the same road as infantry, because it is fatiguing to horses to reduce their rate to that of the foot soldier.

Q. What controls the order of march of the elements of a column?

A. The peculiar conditions under which the march is made, the fundamental principle in all cases being that these elements are arranged from front to rear in the order in which it is likely that they will be most needed. Hence cavalry, as being the most mobile element and the one whose special function it is to give timely notice of the presence of the enemy, should be well advanced to the front. The artillery, which begins the combat, should be so placed as to be able without difficulty to come speedily into action; the engineers should have ample time to remove obstacles and otherwise to further the march of the trops. Lastly, the infantry should be so formed as to assume combat formation with as little delay as possible. Tactical units should, as far as possible, be kept together, and to facilitate the march of large bodies, intervals must be preserved between them.

Q. What is the average rate of marching for the three arms, the world over?

Marches and Supply.

A. For infantry, from 2.75 to 3 miles an hour; for field artillery, 4; for cavalry and horse artillery, 5. These rates assume that men, horses, and roads are in good condition. Moreover, the size of the column affects the rate; other things being equal, a small body will march faster than a large body.

Q. What is the length of an ordinary day's march under favorable conditions?

A. From 12 to 15 miles. At the outset of a campaign, or of a prolonged movement, marches should be, if possible, very short, so as to get the men and horses gradually into condition. It is scarcely necessary to point out that, in any case, the length as well as the rate of a march is influenced by a variety of conditions wholly independent of the character of the troops themselves, such as the weather, the nature of the country, the goodness or badness of the roads, the facilities of supply, etc.

Q. What is meant by a forced march?

A. One in which an extraordinary effort is demanded to carry out some particular object. For large bodies of troops, any march greater than 15 miles a day would be a forced march. It is useless to expect troops not thoroughly trained and disciplined to carry out a forced march.

Q. What circumstances alone will justify a forced march?

A. Extreme necessity, as forced marches seriously injure the fighting powers of even the best troops.

Q. Is continuous marching possible?

A. No; hence all columns on the march halt for a few minutes, generally ten, each hour, and for a longer time once or twice during a longer march. In prolonged movements, it is found necessary to halt for a whole day at intervals, in order to recruit the strength of men and of horses, and to repair material.

Q. What considerations affect the choice of a spot for a long halt?

A. The season of the year, and the weather. Shelter must be sought from wind and rain, and, in any case, an ample supply of water must be readily accessible.

Q. How should troops on the march be quartered at night?

A. If possible, in cantonments; that is, under roof. Under certain circumstances a bivouac in the open is unavoidable, but the proverb always holds that a bad cantonment is better than the best bivouac. A roof not only protects from wind and rain, but enables the men to cook and to eat in comfort.

Q. How may the fatigues of a march be greatly lessened?

A. By requiring all the elements of one and the same column to preserve a uniform pace, and by discouraging all double time of men and trotting of horses to recover lost distances. The comfort of the men is also greatly increased by paying assiduous attention to apparently minor details, such as regularity of meals, abundance of water, modification of the march formation according to the weather and the season of the year, the condition of clothing and of foot-gear, and by taking care that each man and horse has a good night's rest.

Q. Are night marches ever necessary?

A. They may be made necessary by the need of exceptional haste, or by the operations of the enemy, or by the excessive heat of the day. Under a full or nearly full moon, troops can march almost as fast as by day; but, even under the most favorable circumstances, night marches are usually fatiguing, and should not be undertaken unless fully justified by the circumstances of the case.

Supply.

Q. In what two general ways may an army be subsisted in war?

A. First, the army may live upon the country, supplies being obtained by requisition or by purchase, or by both; second, the army may be subsisted by stores, etc., pushed forward from the rear. In practice, both of these methods are usually followed.

Q. Into what two branches is the subject of supplying modern armies from the rear divided?

A. Into, first, the forwarding of stores, rations, forage, etc., and their collection in large magazines and *dépôts;* and, second, the distribution of these stores from these magazines to the army directly. These two services are, or ought to be, perfectly distinct.

Q. What are the characteristics of each of these two services?

A. The first may be semi-civilian in character. It makes use of any and all means of transportation, as rail, wagon, canals, rivers, and keeps its most advanced *dépôts* or stores within one or two marches of the army. The general rule is that it should follow the movements of the army, keeping as close to it as is consistent with the proper performance of its duties. The second, or transportation department distributing directly to the army, must be under perfect military control. It is in contact with the army in front, and with the supply service in rear.

Q. What further element is needed to complete the distribution of supplies to the regiments and other subordinate units?

A. A train of wagons to take the stores and supplies generally as they are brought to the army, and carry them to the respective regiments.

Q. How is the supply service organized in the United States Army?

A. In our army, this service is performed by the Commissary and by the Quartermaster Departments, respectively. The first purchases the supplies, and the second is responsible for their transportation to the armies in the field. These, as we have seen, have as part of their organization wagon trains by which supplies are brought to the armies directly; these wagon trains, however, being operated by the Quartermaster Department under the orders of the general commanding the unit to which they belong.

www.ingramcontent.com/pod-product-compliance
Lightning Source LLC
Chambersburg PA
CBHW031816220426
43662CB00007B/676